Antenna for Social Innovation

Pathways to systemic change

Inspiring stories and a new set of variables for understanding social innovation

Heloise Buckland and David Murillo

Greenleaf
PUBLISHING

© Heloise Buckland and David Murillo
February 2013

Design: www.cosmic.es
Cover photo: Alexis Urusoff and Brewbooks

Published by Greenleaf Publishing Limited
Aizlewood's Mill
Nursery Street
Sheffield S3 8GG
UK
www.greenleaf-publishing.com

Printed in the UK on environmentally friendly, acid-free paper
from managed forests by CPI Group (UK) Ltd, Croydon

British Library Cataloguing in Publication Data:
A catalogue record for this book is available from the British Library.

ISBN: 978-1-78353-053-3 (paperback)
ISBN: 978-1-78353-054-0 (PDF ebook)

Contents

0

Preface and introduction

This book has been inspired by a desire to deepen our understanding of social innovation and its role in addressing today's most pressing social, economic and environmental challenges. The growing movement of what can be succinctly described as "new ideas that solve social problems" is evolving at an unforeseen pace and we are witnessing an unprecedented increase in the volume of social innovations as well as the types of approach taken. In this book we begin by defining a series of variables to help analyse how, when and why social innovation can be most effective. Then, using these variables we go on to analyse four inspiring examples of social innovation. Drawing on this analysis, we conclude by offering some reflections and insights on the key parameters that help identify those social innovations that have the potential to bring about the much needed systemic change to resolve today's challenges.

Building on a track record of research and education in corporate social responsibility and social entrepreneurship in 2011 the Institute of Social Innovation launched the Antenna for Social Innovation with the publication of a report which set out to inspire and raise awareness about the potential for social innovation and to identify global trends and changes in this evolving sector. The broad overview offered by this initial report was accompanied by critical reflections on core debates concerning, firstly, the definitions and characteristics of social innovation, and, secondly, the challenges faced by social entrepreneurs and the social contexts in which they operate. In this first report we used social innovation as an overarching term to encompass social entrepreneurship, social enterprise, philanthropy and a series of different, primarily private, initiatives that work towards bringing solutions to pressing social problems.

Ten inspiring social innovations from around the world were highlighted in the first report which concluded that the sector is gaining momentum. Indeed, this is evident from the sheer volume of initiatives, from grassroots community projects and innovative private initiatives to paradigm-shifting regional and global networks for change. Furthermore, the increasing prominence of what have become known as Innovation HUBS also reflects a growing interest in stimulating and supporting these innovations. These HUBS, which provide emerging support systems for social entrepreneurs and new innovations, include academic centres, organisations and foundations, governments and international sharing platforms.

Building on our understanding of some of the key characteristics and challenges faced by social entrepreneurs, in this year's report we present five key variables to enable a deeper analysis of social innovation. These variables cover a range of aspects including the level of social transformation achieved, the strategies deployed to work across sectors and boundaries, financial stability and viability, the types of innovation adopted and finally, the potential to scale or replicate initiatives.

We have selected four remarkable initiatives each operating at a very different scale (urban, regional, national and international) and their stories are explored through the lens of five variables. While each case is an inspiring example of social innovation in itself, considering them all as a group contributes to a deeper understanding of how best to measure social innovation and identify future challenges and success factors.

Our selection of case studies and variables is by no means random. Through the analysis of these cases we are convinced that we can all learn from the globalised and open environment in which social innovation operates. Furthermore, the relationship between global and local initiatives is bi-directional: we learn from what is happening beyond our political borders by incorporating, translating and adapting what functions well far from here, while also sharing via the internet, through publications, reports and case studies what we have learned about social innovation, thereby transferring it to the global sphere.

In terms of the chosen variables each is significant. To begin with, we should declare our point of departure: there is no one definition of social innovation, nor will there ever be. The debate concerning the precision of terminology may be of interest to academics and experts, but when we engage with practitioners, who may potentially be interested in this type of publication, such debates are at best of secondary interest. What interests us is what each of us understands by social innovation, and above all, according to what variables can we think about it, analyse it and transmit it.

Our selection is based on what we understand as the pressing issues affecting our immediate context. We are in need of tried-and-tested initiatives that function: that is to say, which provide some type of measurable (local or global) social impact, and which are efficient and results oriented. Therefore, they must be initiatives that are willing to cross sectors and management styles (public, private, non-profit) and to take from each of these spheres whatever they can benefit. Furthermore they must be open initiatives, replicable and at least to a certain degree scalable. In other words they should be transferable: ones that we can teach about, share and learn from the analysis of their way of working in a way that goes beyond their local and specific reality. Finally, and of special relevance for the present economic climate, they have to be self-sufficient initiatives, independent of the pull of the public sector and in their use of public funding.

A final point regarding how to read this book: fans of the writing of Julio Cortázar will recall the introduction to Rayuela (1963) and the different itineraries the author designed for the reading of his work. There are also different ways to engage with the content of this book. We would like to propose three:

A. Those interested in gaining an understanding of what social innovation is in practice can go directly to the book's third section, which is devoted to the four case studies. They can choose the case study that interests them on the basis of the profile of its instigators (NGO, government or civil society) or the project's scope (global, national, regional or local). A brief reading of the introduction of each case study should suffice for the reader to understand the central characteristics of each one prior to immersing themselves in the transversal analysis of the different variables undertaken for each case study.

B. For those interested in the theoretical debate concerning social innovation, we believe that this study provides a relevant contribution to it through its in-depth examination of the different variables and dimensions. Sections 1 and 3 offer an introduction to and analysis of the literature published on each of the variables presented. Then in Section 4 a review of this is offered in the light of the case studies examined.

C. Finally, the traditional way of reading can follow the book's established order: beginning with the introduction of the variables analysed (Section 1), then addressing their use in the different case studies (Section 2), going on to see these variables' development in the specific literature (Section 3) and finally a re-reading of them on the basis of the principal ideas acquired from the case studies (Section 4). The appendices are for those interested in a more transversal perspective of the different definitions of social innovation and the principal promotional agents.

We would like especially to express our gratitude to the teams working at Avaaz, the Behavioural Insights Team, Barcelona Food Bank and the Barcelona Exchange Networks, who by sharing their experiences and challenges with us have made this publication possible. We hope their stories serve both to inspire others and to offer insight into the potential that exists for finding new ways of solving today's most pressing challenges.

Heloise Buckland and David Murillo
February 2013

1

Social innovation variables

The increasing demand for innovative approaches to solve complex environmental, social and economic challenges is being met by individuals and organisations from all walks of life across the planet. A wealth of support mechanisms has emerged to accompany the growing activity of social innovators: these include diverse sources of funding, international sharing platforms, incubators, research programmes and networks. Coupled with this growing interest in social innovation there is also an increasing demand for mechanisms to identify the types of approaches that are most effective and measure their impact and long-term viability.

The following five variables have been selected to contribute to the global debate about what social innovation means, where its boundaries lie, how its impact can be measured and finally, what the key factors for success are for any given initiative.

Table 1. Five variables to analyse social innovation

	VARIABLE	QUESTIONS THAT ARISE
1	**Social transformation and impact**	How effective is the initiative at achieving the desired social transformation, and resolving the problem it set out to address?
2	**Cross-sector collaboration**	Who are the key stakeholders in ensuring that the initiative is successful and what are the mechanisms used to engage with them?
3	**Economic sustainability and long-term viability**	How is the initiative funded and what are the strategies adopted to ensure its survival in the future?
4	**Innovation type**	Is the innovation closed or open to be replicated by others? Is the idea developed from an earlier concept and what are its innovative characteristics?
5	**Scalability and replicability**	What is the potential for the initiative to expand or multiply and what conditions are required for it to be replicated in a different situation?

Why these variables?

Much of the thinking around social innovation is focused on measuring the impact of each innovation which seeks to establish to what degree a particular innovation achieves its objectives, what results it achieves and how effective it is at an organisational level. Given that the overarching aim of any social innovation is to achieve a specific social goal, there is a general consensus that measuring the extent to which that goal is reached should be a priority. In other words, there is a focus on measuring *results*. However, there is less agreement around how to measure the *processes* adopted to achieve the stated goals, which includes issues such as: which partnership models work best; how economic viability can be achieved; whether open or closed innovation is more effective and, finally; what conditions are necessary for scaling an initiative.

The five variables offered here aim to cover both a results-oriented and a process-oriented perspective to provide a more holistic lens through which to observe different social innovations and better understand their potential.

Who measures social innovation?

There are a number of stakeholders who already use a series of mechanisms to evaluate social innovation, most with a focus on a given initiative's potential for growth and long-term viability. We have grouped them into the following four categories.

Investors. A key group is the growing community of socially responsible investors. These include fund managers seeking viable investments to complete their socially responsible investment (SRI) portfolio, social impact investors such as the Acumen Fund, banks with a clear ethical policy such as Triodos and financial sector networks such as the European Social Investment Forum.

Foundations and organisations. Notable philanthropic institutions that support social entrepreneurs include the Young Foundation, the Skoll Foundation (in partnership with The University of Oxford's Saïd Business School), the Social Innovation Forum and Ashoka. The Schwab Foundation and the Kellogg Foundation are two other leading entities that seek to identify social entrepreneurs with the potential to bring about social change and support them financially. These organisations use increasingly sophisticated selection processes to assess the potential of individual entrepreneurs and the innovations that they support.

Academic centres. Another sector actively involved in the research and development of mechanisms to analyse social innovation are business schools and universities; leading examples include the Center for Social Innovation at the Stanford Graduate School of Business, The University of Oxford's Saïd Business School and Harvard Business School. As well as social innovation being a dimension of their research activity, a number of these institutions are now integrating it into their teaching. Furthermore, some are adopting action-based research approaches or incubating budding social entrepreneurs, as is the case with ESADE's Momentum Project and INSEAD's Social Innovation Centre's outreach programme.

Governments. Many public organisations actively seek out social innovation as a new way of delivering social and environmental services, from renewable energy to childcare, particularly in a context of increasing financial strain on the public purse. On the one hand, governments may support individual social innovations to meet the demand for a particular social service or, on the other, they may work in collaboration with the business and non-profit sector to develop more effective solutions to a given social problem. In either case, there is increasing interest from public organisations in being able to identify and evaluate different types of social innovation.

Five social innovation variables

The discussion that follows outlines the reasoning behind the selection of these social innovation variables. Drawing on the analysis of the four social innovation initiatives in this report, the conceptual framework and thinking behind each of these variables is further explored in Chapter 4.

Social transformation and impact. Regardless of the definition of social innovation, there is a consensus that any one social innovation aims to address one or more *social* problems. For the purposes of this report, we use *social* as an overarching term to encompass specific environmental, economic or ethical challenges, or, as is most commonly the case, a particular problem that has these three dimensions. How to measure this social impact or evaluate social transformation is an area of research where most effort has been devoted to reporting techniques, performance measurement and indicator development. How well an initiative is achieving its objective is therefore clearly an important variable to consider.

Cross-sector collaboration. A social innovation rarely operates in isolation and this is ever more the case in the network age, where the boundaries between the private, public, collective and individual spheres are increasingly blurred. Traditional hierarchies are being reconstructed at many levels and there are many spaces and forums where businesses, governments and civil society cooperate to redress gaps in the provision of social and environmental products and services. The points of entry for collaboration and the motivations for different sectors or different types of stakeholder can vary for each type of social innovation and the new landscape of hybrid organisations is of special interest.

Economic sustainability and long-term viability. While there is no single definition of a social enterprise, there is a common understanding that this type of organisation differs from a traditional non-profit organisation or charity in having a greater focus on self-sufficiency and performance-driven results. Key dimensions to consider include investment versus payback time, efficiency and effectiveness and a management capacity to enable long-term viability. Innovation in fundraising techniques, low-cost implementation strategies and challenges to growth are also key factors to consider.

Innovation type. Broadly speaking, social innovations are of two types. First, those based on open innovation, where users and stakeholders are free to copy, reuse and adapt an idea. Closed innovation models are based on the concept of intellectual property where the knowledge is kept within the hands of the creator. While there is a general shift towards open-source solutions and peer-to-peer development, it is not necessarily the most suitable solution to achieve a desired social impact. The relationship between the type of innovation and its scalability and replicability is also an interesting variable to explore.

Scalability and replicability. The capacity for social innovation to be increased or reduced in scale or to be replicated is significant for two reasons. Firstly, as many of our current social and environmental problems are global, such as climate change, desertification, the depletion of our ocean's reserves and mass migrations, solutions are required on a global scale. Secondly, as many of aspects of society have been globalised, such as the financial sector or multinational enterprises, and individual countries increasingly operate at an international level, as is the case with the European Union or NAFTA, what works in one nation or even one city can often be adapted to another. The same is true of social innovation.

2

Four inspiring examples of social innovation

In this chapter we focus on four very different examples of social innovation. These have been selected both to demonstrate the enormous diversity of types of social innovation that exist today, and to test the value of the five chosen variables as significant parameters for analysing any given initiative. The cases include the world's largest global online social and environmental activism community, a hub for local networks that exchange goods and services without using money, a food bank specialised in avoiding food wastage by redistributing it to those in need and, finally, a government unit whose mission is to integrate behavioural economics into public policy to enhance social welfare.

To analyse these four examples, a systematic qualitative approach has been adopted, based on semi-structured interviews with a select group of key stakeholders for each organisation. Where possible, the founders of the initiative have been interviewed. The interviews have been complemented by a review of internal documentation, websites, financial reports and other publications as well as articles and reports about each case study from third parties. Table 2 provides a summary of the four case studies.

Table 2. Summary of four examples of social innovation

INITIATIVE	MISSION	MECHANISM	FOUNDED	SCALE
Avaaz	Organise citizens of all nations to close the gap between the world we have and the world most people everywhere want.	Global web movement and direct action to bring people-powered politics to decision making.	2006	Global, with 20 million members in 194 countries.
Barcelona Food Bank	Fight poverty and food waste.	Collection and redistribution of food to urban poor with annual collection campaign.	1987	Local, mobilising 7,600 volunteers, 600 organisations across Catalonia.
Behavioural Insights Team	Find innovative, cost effective ways to enable citizens to make better choices.	Unit within central UK government applying behavioural economics to public policy.	2010	National, with activity across the UK and potential for replication.
Barcelona exchange networks	Exchange goods and services and create support networks in urban areas.	Self-organised neighbourhood exchange systems that do not use money.	1992	Urban, operating in 8 neighbourhoods in Barcelona.

Diversity of scope

The four examples all illustrate the succinct definition of social innovation offered by the Skoll Centre for Social Entrepreneurship at the Saïd Business School : "*new ideas that work in meeting social goals*" (Mulgan *et al.* 2007: 8).[1] Given that social needs and problems, whether at a domestic or global level, manifest themselves in many different ways, innovative responses to them also demonstrate an incredible diversity of approaches. For this reason the case studies selected range from a global, 20 million strong citizens' movement for tackling international issues such as European policy on GMOs and ocean protection, to a network of neighbourhood exchange schemes focused on building community resilience from street level upwards. The other two cases focus on nationwide and urban issues respectively.

Diversity of sector

Traditionally, social innovation was understood as the social sector filling the gap in public service provision (e.g. Health Leeds, Year Up, Ashoka, Echoing Green and New Profit). However, there is an emerging view that the public sector should take on elements of social innovation to enhance its delivery of services (Hecht 2012).[2] For this reason one of the cases selected is the integration of behavioural economics in public policy led by the UK Government Cabinet Office's Behavioural Insights Team. According to Hecht, CEO of Living Cities, "*public sector innovation is undertaken with the assumption that if it is successful, it will go 'intravenously' into effect, with no fundraising or advocacy needed.*"[3] While the other case studies are civil society led, they have very different organisational cultures. For example, although Avaaz is a non-profit organisation, its founder was inspired by companies such as Walmart and Apple, and it has a very different culture from the local exchange networks, which are organic non-formalised organisms, or the Barcelona Food Bank, which is a traditional private foundation with a classic hierarchical structure.

---

1 Mulgan, G., Tucker, S. , Ali, R., & Sanders, B. (2007) *Social Innovation: What it is, why it matters and how it can be accelerated.* Oxford Saïd Business School, Skoll Centre for Entrepreneurship. London.

2 Ben Hecht, "Mainstreaming Social Innovation with the Public Sector", published in the *Huffington Post*, 16th April 2012.

3 This was the concept behind the Centre for Economic Opportunity (CEO) to design and implement evidence-based initiatives to reduce poverty and which has already developed measures that have been adopted by the Obama administration.

Diversity of approach

The Social Innovation Exchange[4] describes social innovation as "the development and implementation of new ideas (products, services and models) to meet social needs." The cases studied in this book use very different mechanisms to achieve their social goals, ranging from online petitions to organising volunteers to man supermarket food collection points, neighbourhood swap markets to knowledge exchange systems and even applying behavioural science to policy-making. The mechanisms used, the financial incentives and the human resources management are different in every case. For example, one organisation operates with 180 regular volunteers, another with 8 full-time civil servants, another with staff based in 18 countries, mostly working online from their own homes.

Diversity of social innovation phases

Each case is at a slightly different phase in their development, which provides another interesting dimension. Avaaz, having grown to 20 million members and with offices in 18 countries, has clearly gone well into the stage of scaling up its operations, whereas the Behavioural Insights Team is just half way through a pilot-testing phase. The exchange networks in Barcelona are sustaining their momentum, but are yet to scale up their activity to a city-wide effort and the Barcelona Food Bank is perhaps at a tipping point of scaling up its operations with the potential to engage in a nationwide scheme.

Figure 1. Social innovation spiral

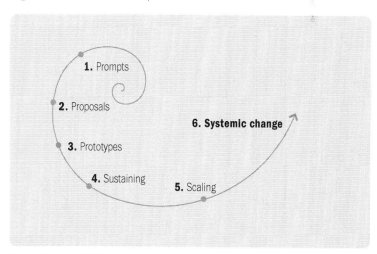

Source: Murray et al. 2010

Avaaz

«A campaigning community bringing people-powered politics to decision-making worldwide – the largest global web movement in history.»
—**Avaaz**

Mission	Organise citizens of all nations to close the gap between the world we have and the world most people everywhere want.
Founded	2006
Scalability	Global with members in 194 countries.
Location	Main office in New York, with campaigners in more than 18 countries.
Financing	Since 2010 Avaaz has been funded entirely by individual donations. The average sum donated is €25.
Social impact	Global, regional, national and local (depending on the focus of each campaign).
Open innovation	No
Innovation	Leveraging a massive global community for change on a global scale.

Introduction

Avaaz is a global community of individuals who are mobilised to support social change through an online platform. To date, 20 million people have signed up to Avaaz, supporting online petitions for a variety of social and environmental causes as well as participating in direct action campaigns across the world. This section gives an overview of Avaaz, why it was set up, who supports the movement and how and where its efforts are focused.

«Avaaz is an ally, and a rallying place, for disadvantaged people everywhere to help create real change.»
—**Zainab Bangura, foreign minister of Sierra Leone**[5]

Why Avaaz?

Avaaz means "voice" or "song" in several languages including Hindi, Urdu, Nepali, Turkish, Farsi and Bosnian. It was co-founded in 2006 by Res Publica, a global civic advocacy group and moveon.org, an online community that has pioneered internet advocacy in the United States. The co-founding team comprised a group of six leading social entrepreneurs from six different countries.

Since the outset, Avaaz's mission has been to "*organise citizens of all nations to close the gap between the world we have and the world most people everywhere want*". Through its online platform, Avaaz aims to

5 www.avaaz.org, accessed 12th December 2011.

rapidly combine the efforts of millions of individuals into a powerful collective voice for effecting change on pressing global, regional and national issues. The underlying philosophy is:

> «to ensure that the views and values of the world's people inform the decisions that affect us all»
> —**Avaaz** [6]

Avaaz was set up in recognition of the many movements, coalitions and organisations that have over time fragmented into smaller entities due to the difficulty of building consensus on specific issues. Instead of striving for a consensus on any single issue, Avaaz organises a wide selection of campaigns enabling each individual to choose whether or not to participate. However, experience shows that once people join the community through one campaign, they more often than not go on to take action on another issue and then another, thus strengthening the community and its capacity to act.

Who makes up the community?

Avaaz, with its website translated into 15 languages, currently has over 20 million members who come from 194 countries, and membership is growing fast. In Brazil, France and Germany Avaaz has more than one million members and in France, Germany, Italy, Spain and Canada members represent over 1% of the total population. The community is divided roughly equally between young, middle-aged and elderly people from different walks of life, including professionals, the unemployed, students and retired members. Just over half of these are women.

Table 3. Avaaz membership in numbers

COUNTRY	% OF POPULATION	MEMBERS
Germany	2,0%	1,174,478
France	1,7%	1,185,127
Canada	1,7%	576,176
Spain	1,4%	675,741
Italy	1,2%	726,780
Brazil	0,6%	1,323,420
US	0,2%	899,746
Mexico	0,3%	359,682
India	0,06%	831,417

Source: www.avaaz.org, accessed 25th February 2012

---

6 www.avaaz.org, accessed 12th December 2011.

How does the movement work?

A core team of 60 people work from 18 countries including Australia, Japan, India, Russia, Israel, Lebanon, Italy, Switzerland, Germany, France, UK, Spain, Colombia, Brazil, US, Canada and Sweden using online tools to collaborate in a virtual office. This team is supported by a network of thousands of volunteers in different parts of the world and, since 2007, it has run over 1,000 campaigns on a diverse set of issues.

At any one time there are seven to eight campaigns actively being promoted on their website covering a range of social and environmental challenges from an international, regional or local perspective. Previous campaigns have been organised into ten thematic areas: emergency response, climate change, corruption, human rights, natural world, Burma, Tibet, peace, food and farms, media and the internet.

Many of the campaigns are organised through online petitions delivered to key decision-makers and politicians around the world. Typically, around 500,000 people will sign any one petition and, in some cases, targets have reached 3 million, as is the case of the Save the Internet campaign. Since 2007, 15 million signatures have been gathered for the area of climate change alone. The Avaaz community also organises a series of direct action activities, including demonstrations, crowdsourcing, secret safe houses, phone and messaging campaigns, press advertisements, banners, T-shirt campaigns and emergency aid donations. A total of 69,655,629 actions have been taken since 2007.[7]

«We're not just effectively delivering petitions, we're running safe houses and smuggling routes to protect democratic movements, challenging corporations by bringing lawsuits or calling all their shareholders, donating millions to equip human rights defenders with the latest technology, and powerfully delivering the voices of our community direct and in person to presidents, billionaires, ambassadors and cabinet ministers.»
—**Ricken Patel** [8]

Achievements so far

Building the community to a scale where it has the ability to make a significant difference on any urgent issue that citizens care about has been one of Avaaz's primary objectives since it was founded. This section gives an overview of Avaaz's greatest achievements so far and highlights from 2011.

«The creation of the community itself and its potential promise for the future is our greatest achievement so far. The creation of the network and all of its potential it one of the things I'm most excited about – the scale, breadth, diversity, level of engagement, willingness to donate and to go offline.»
—**Ricken Patel** [9]

Since 2007, Avaaz has carried out over 50 million actions online and offline to influence public policy respond to emergencies and support citizen's movements across the world. In addition to the messages sent, phone calls and petition signatures, Avaaz has organised almost 10,000 rallies, flash mobs, vigils

7 www.avaaz.org, accessed 12th December 2011.

8 Extract from email to Avaaz members from Executive Director Ricken Patel, December 2011.

9 Interview with Ricken Patel, 9th December 2011.

marches and other events, giving a massive boost to the climate change movement and other vital campaigns (Avaaz).[10] Examples of significant achievements have been made in the following three arenas.

Influencing public policy

An area of outstanding progress has been the contribution to anti-corruption legislation. Avaaz's efforts were considered to have made a significant contribution in the adoption of new anti-corruption legislation known as "Ficha Limpa" (or "Clean Record" in English) in Brazil and "Jan Lokpal" in India. An unprecedented 700,000 people signed Avaaz's petition supporting this new anti-corruption law in India. Avaaz has also successfully targeted its efforts to halting unpopular political action, such as Berlusconi's proposed censorship legislation and Uganda's Anti-Gay Bill. In the UK, Canada and Australia Avaaz has successfully influenced respective governments to stop the media giant Rupert Murdoch's plans to create a monopoly for his media group: in the UK the government halted the acquisition of BSkyB, in Canada the purchase of a major TV network was denied, and in Australia the authorities have agreed to undertake a media reform and enquiry into Murdoch's operations.

Figure 2. Avaaz Murdoch Campaign

Avaaz demonstration in April 2012 outside the Royal Courts of Justice in London during the Leveson Inquiry into Rupert and James Murdoch's business practices.

---

10 www.avaaz.org, accessed 12th January 2012.

Responding to emergencies

Human rights and democracy advocates in Burma, Zimbabwe, Tibet, Iran, Egypt and Syria as well as other countries have been supported by Avaaz in emergency situations with funding for high-technology means of communication, practical resources such as fuel, vehicles and medical supplies as well as with help in smuggling activists out of a country or providing them with safe houses. In 2011, Avaaz responded to the "Arab Spring" uprisings with its successful and still ongoing campaign "Break the Blackout", which supports a citizen journalists' network, delivers emergency aid to the countries involved and helps activists on the ground. Funds have also been raised and effectively delivered to victims of natural disasters such as the cyclone in Burma, the earthquake in Haiti and floods in Pakistan.

Supporting global citizen's movements

Avaaz has supported citizen's movements around the world on a wide variety of issues. At an international level, significant areas of achievement include climate change, where multiple petitions have been signed in partnership with numerous NGOs and climate advocacy groups. Other victories include work with advocacy groups to help establish one of the largest marine reserves in the world, defence of the international ban on cluster bombs and the bans on whaling and the ivory trade. Avaaz has also supported indigenous movements. In one case, hundreds of indigenous protestors in Bolivia were supported by a petition from Avaaz to halt the construction of a highway through a national park. In Brazil, Avaaz has joined indigenous groups and activists in their struggle to stop the Belo Monte dam and reverse deforestation in the Amazon.

Figure 3. Avaaz Petition against whaling

The delivery of Avaaz's petition to Romulo José Fernandes Barreto Mello and Fabia de Oliveira Luna from the Brazil delegation at the International Whaling Commission in Agadir, Morocco, June 2010.

Table 4. Highlights of Avaaz 2011 activities

CAMPAIGNS	ACTION TAKEN	RESULTS
On the front line of the Arab Spring	$1.5m raised for a citizens' media network, $1m delivered in emergency relief, activists smuggled out or kept in secret safe houses. 600,000 messages broadcast in Tahrir Square, 500,000 signatures to stop Mubarak's fortune leaving the country.	Heightened international media coverage of Arab Spring, Mubarak's assets frozen and hundreds of activists and their families helped.
People power versus Murdoch Mafia	668,784 messages and 30,000 phone calls to members of the UK parliament to stop Murdoch acquiring BSkyB. Media stunts, opinion polls and shareholder campaigns in Australia to stop acquisition of a $223 million TV contract from the public broadcaster.	UK government halts Murdoch's acquisition plans and Australian government initiates an inquiry into Murdoch and media reform.
Global outcry to save the Amazon	500,000 signatures to support 1,000 indigenous protestors to halt construction of a highway through the TIPNI National Park in Bolivia, Amazon region. The petition was delivered personally to office of president Evo Morales by Avaaz staff.	Morales halted construction plans and pledges to protect the National Park forever.
Victory on Cluster Bombs	600,000 signatures helped push 50 states to oppose the US's plan of revoking the global ban on cluster bombs. A powerful banner and 1,000 fliers handed out at the conference centre where the treaty was being debated sent an unequivocal reminder to the negotiators of grassroots opposition to the ban being revoked.	Many delegates used the petition to strengthen their arguments against the revocation of the ban, which was finally rejected.
Climate Change: Keeping Hope Alive	800,000 Avaaz protesters put the pressure on at the Durban Climate Change talks and their views were accompanied by the release of adverts in the *Financial Times* on the final day of negotiations when a deal was finally struck to save the Kyoto Protocol.	Talks salvaged on the last day with an agreement to work on a deal that will have legal force and will come into effect in 2015.
Taking on corruption in India	In 36 hours, over 700,000 Indians joined the petition to support a new anti-corruption law, "Jan Lokpal". Marches, hard-hitting billboards across the Indian capital, and an independent public opinion poll showing that the majority of Indian voters wanted the "Jan Lokpal" to be an ambitious piece of legislation.	Government moves forward on draft anti-corruption bill to deter corruption, redress grievances, and protect whistle-blowers.
Italy wins freedom of speech	200,000 emails sent, Facebook and Twitter flooded with messages and hard-hitting public demonstrations covered by top media were all used to stop the law on internet censorship proposed by Berlusconi during the final months of his leadership.	Berlusconi's proposal to be able to shut down internet websites rejected by parliament.

Impact and degree of transformation

What is Avaaz's social impact, and to what degree have the campaigns achieved a real transformation? This section demonstrates the ways in which Avaaz has been able to measure, and above all communicate, the impact its campaigns are having on the social injustices and environmental abuses it targets, as well as the degree to which it is achieving its mission.

> «Avaaz is inspiring... it has already made a significant difference.»
> —**Al Gore**[11]

Moments of global togetherness

Today, Avaaz is considered the largest web movement in history. The sheer volume of traffic generated by the site, with over 20 million users, has produced unprecedented potential to create a visible impact on almost any issue considered important by its members. In addition to this it has formed an especially diverse community, with members from almost all countries around the world, which has the capacity to make citizens' voices heard on a multitude of issues. The most commonly used mechanism to channel these individuals' voices is by circulating petitions and carrying out fundraising in very short spaces of time, such as collecting typically around 500,000 signatures in just a few days. Once the signatures have been collected, the petitions are then delivered to the relevant political leader in a high-visibility media event.

> «Avaaz harnesses the increasing incidents of moments of global togetherness, where the entire world comes together and wants action on a particular issue. We collect the energy of these moments into a vessel that can then be deployed time and time again much more effectively and much more rapidly than before.»
> —**Ricken Patel**[12]

Fundraising and targeted relief

The strength in numbers of the Avaaz community has enabled highly effective fundraising, not just in terms of volume (over $20 million has been raised online since 2007), but also in terms of the speed with which funds have been raised and successfully delivered to the people in need. A good example of this is the case of the Burma cyclone where Avaaz raised $2m in one week and delivered the aid directly to the victims. In a context where traditional international aid was being either blocked by the military regime, siphoned off in border taxes of up to 40% or diverted to regions not affected by the cyclone, Avaaz managed to get funds directly to the most affected Delta region within days of the disaster. Having already worked with Burmese monks in 2007 when $350,000 was delivered to support communication technologies, Avaaz activated previously used online money transfer mechanisms and existing connections with the monks who were able to buy fuel vehicles, medicine and other key supplies for the monasteries where people were being housed

---

11 www.avaaz.org, accessed 25th February 2012.

12 Interview with Ricken Patel, 9th December 2012.

after the cyclone. Similar campaigns have been run in other countries including Haiti and Pakistan where, almost overnight, the community has raised funds and through a sophisticated system of global networks and trusted local partners money has been delivered to those in need effectively and on time.

International media coverage

At the time of writing, Avaaz generates 3,6 million results on Google and is frequently mentioned in mainstream international media, For example, 174 articles referring to the platform have been published in the *New York Times*, 163 in the *Guardian*, 49 on the BBC website and 27 on CNN.[13] It also has a significant presence in independent media channels. Presence in the media highlights the increasing recognition Avaaz is gaining as a key player in global advocacy. Numerous blogs make reference to Syrian state TV calling Avaaz campaigner Wissam Tarif *"the most dangerous man in the world"* to the regime, the *Times of India* hailed Avaaz as *"a key player in the Jan Lokpal initiative"*,[14] *Le Monde* called the *Ficha Limpa* campaign in Brazil an *"impressive and unprecedented petition campaign"* and a *"spectacular political and moral victory for civil society"*, and *Time* magazine has recently published an article entitled "How a New York City based Activist has become a player in Syria".[15]

Politicians have also recognised the role of Avaaz. EU Commissioner for Climate Action Connie Hedegaard stated after the Durban climate talks: *"Thanks to the over 800,000 people from around the world – your voices made a vital impact at the end of the talks."*[16]

In addition to the coverage given to its campaigns by international and national media organisations, Avaaz has also taken a proactive approach to media promotion by crowdfunding adverts in newspapers and other press channels. For example, a full page "Cli-Matrix" advertisement in the *Financial Times* was delivered to delegates at the Copenhagen Climate Change summit, portraying world leaders as film heroes and exhorting them to *"fund the fight to save the world"*. At the height of the 2007 UN climate negotiations in Bali, a full-page Avaaz advertisement in the *Jakarta Post* was waved at a pivotal Japanese cabinet meeting; the Environment Minister held up the advertisement and asked the Prime Minister, *"are we letting the world see Japan as blocking targets for 2020?"*[17] During the same summit, one of the largest online actions in Canadian history and a national advertising campaign prompted a U-turn on targets for cutting dangerous planet-warming emissions. Canada's opposition leader exclaimed in response, *"Avaaz members, reversing the bad policy of a government, this is great... join Avaaz, because it works."* Similarly an advertisement was sponsored by Avaaz members on the last day of Durban climate talks in 2011.

During the Hokkaido G8 summit in July 2008, a full-page satirical advertisement based on the Japanese cartoon character Hello Kitty showing the faces of the Japanese and Canadian Prime Ministers Yasuo Fukuda and Stephen Harper with US President George Bush was featured in the *New York Times* (Figure 4).

---

13 Figures compiled from searches of the *New York Times*, *Guardian*, BBC and CNN websites on 25th February 2012.

14 "Indian origin Canadian is voice of Jan Lokpal", article published in *Times of India*, 11th August 2011.

15 "How a New York City based Activist has become a player in Syria", published in *Time* magazine, 15th March 2012.

16 Inewp.com, "The People's Press", 11th December 2011.

17 *Asahi Simbun Newspaper*: www.asahi.com.

Other media organisations including the Canadian Broadcasting Corporation and Nikkei Business Daily subsequently commented on the advertisement.[18]

Figure 4. Avaaz advertisement in the *Financial Times*

Avaaz has also used television advertising to gain support for its campaigns. Back in January 2007, when many leaders refused to recognise the threat of catastrophic climate change an Avaaz TV advertisement was launched on four continents to help disseminate information about the role of oil companies in blocking global climate change agreements. Another good example of this tactic is a 2009 campaign launched at the height of fossil fuel companies lobbying the US government to prevent a strict global climate treaty. Avaaz members also funded an advertisement on Washington DC television spoofing ExxonMobil's environmental adverts, which triggered a response from the company.

18 "Richest nations pledge to half greenhouse gases", published in *New York Times*, 9th July 2008. See Figure 4.

Nimbleness and flexibility

«Previous international citizens' groups and social movements have had to build a constituency for each separate issue, year by year and country by country, in order to reach a scale that could make a difference. Today, thanks to new technology and a rising ethic of global interdependence, that constraint no longer applies.»

—**Avaaz**[19]

The speed and accessibility of the internet, social networks and new technologies and the rising ethic of global interdependence has enabled Avaaz to grow exponentially in the last five years of its history. The structure of the organisation is a single global team with a mandate to work on any issue of public concern with small teams of campaigners. These lead all aspects of the campaign from fundraising to communication which means that work is delivered with incredible focus and speed. Rather than the typical structure of a large NGO with national chapters each with their own staff, budget and decision-making procedures, bureaucratic structures and processes built around internal communication, fundraising and marketing departments, in Avaaz the campaign teams are autonomous. They are responsible for every part of their campaign. This not only means that they can focus on the job in hand, but as individuals on the front line they are also the people best informed to deal with the media, communicate clear messages for fundraising or react to unpredicted events.

Avaaz's nimbleness translates into rapid fundraising and petition signing and is also a sophisticated blend of online and offline activity. For example, during the *Ficha Limpa* campaign in Brazil, in parallel to collecting signatures for the online petition, Avaaz members were also present at the negotiations themselves to identify those politicians opposing the proposed legislation, so that immediately after the meetings they could rally Avaaz supporters to target them with phone calls and emails to persuade them to back the law. Receiving this kind of targeted pressure from their own constituents, above all in real time, was unprecedented for Brazilian politicians.

«Avaaz's online community can act like a megaphone to call attention to new issues; a lightning rod to channel broad public concern into a specific, targeted campaign; a fire truck to rush an effective response to a sudden, urgent emergency; and a stem cell that grows into whatever form of advocacy or work is best suited to meet an urgent need.»

—**Avaaz**[20]

19 www.avaaz.org, accessed 25th February 2012.
20 www.avaaz.org accessed 12th February 2012.

Winnable battles

A key strategy used by the Avaaz team in order to ensure that their campaigns achieve the desired impact is to identify winnable targets where a difference can be made. It is also important that campaigns can be clearly communicated to members and serve as motivation for continued action. On a practical level, when signing petitions the web page is constantly updated to ensure an ongoing motivation for people to sign up.

«What we do is take really difficult problems and try to crunch them down to find a winnable battle.»
—**Ricken Patel**[21]

At a campaign level, difficult global issues, such as Chinese oppression in Tibet, are broken down into achievable targets to enable progress to be made and to prevent the feeling of helplessness that some global movements face with overambitious aims. In this case, where Avaaz recognises that while it may be extremely difficult to get the Chinese to leave Tibet, it is still possible to shift Chinese policy towards dialogue and to ensure that the Tibetan stories are heard by the rest of the world. One way to help draw media attention to the situation was to send radio equipment, satellite phones and internet networks to the monasteries, and to provide the monks with computers to enable external communication. Another winnable objective was to get major countries to send their diplomats to the area to communicate what is happening to their own constituents and, in turn, send a message to the Chinese that they cannot pursue repression with impunity.

Selected campaigns that will make a difference

Avaaz describes its strategy as "focusing on tipping-point moments of crisis and opportunity" to help select the campaigns that will make a significant difference. Avaaz recognises and builds on the years of campaigning by dedicated groups on individual issues or causes and it is alert to the moment when public attention is attracted to the cause. It is at this moment that the opportunity is greatest for influencing a crucial decision by a key decision-maker. There is a brief window of opportunity to influence that decision and this is where Avaaz makes its mark, rallying support in some cases in less than 24 hours to help influence the decision;

«doing in hours what used to take years»
—**Ricken Patel**[21]

21 Interview with Ricken Patel, 9th December 2011.

In any one country these opportunities may appear once or twice a year. However, given the community's global reach, several may happen each week. This focus on the "tipping points" gives the community a sense of urgency and immediacy which serves to stimulate a quick response from users.

Table 5. Types of campaigns run by Avaaz

TYPE OF CAMPAIGN	OBJECTIVE
Impact	Break down global issues into achievable targets to change the world (one step at a time)
Viral	Increase community membership
Brand	Brand enhancement
Fundraising	Raise funds for a cause
Member service	Give the members opportunities to do something they want to do

Source: Interview with Ricken Patel, 9th December 2011

The process used to select campaigns is a crucial part of the strategy to ensure impact and to achieve transformation. A classification of the different types of campaign, as shown in Table 5, is applied. The organisational-focused campaigns (viral, brand, fundraising) are considered a long-term investment, which ultimately build capacity to make an impact. If a key goal is virality (the capacity to spread widely) and intended to increase Avaaz member numbers, strategies such as a petition will be used followed up by a series of sharing tools. If the aim of the campaign is impact, on the other hand, an approach they may take is to encourage people to write to their politicians. In these cases there will be lower participation and no viral dimension. The team's increasing experience is showing that the best campaigns are the ones that hit all targets – that are popular, build the community and help change the world through achievable targets. Over time, these approaches have been merged and a more holistic approach appears to be the most successful way to select the campaigns that will make a difference.

Table 6. Key characteristics of Avaaz's impact in target areas

CAMPAIGN	YEAR	OBJECTIVE	NUMBERS	RESULTS
Iraq	2007	Withdrawal of US troops from Iraq.	150,000 signatures.	Contribution to the petition for autonomy of Iraqi people handed over to world leaders.
Amazon	2009	Against the increase of agro-business in the Amazon.	14,000 poll participants and 30,000 messages submitted to President Lula.	Legislation permitting agricultural exploitation of the Amazon revoked.
Sakineh Ashtiani	2010	Appeal against death penalty of Sakineh an Iranian woman accused of adultery.	More than 900,000 messages sent to Turkish and Brazilian governments.	Sakineh released from death row. President Lula offered her asylum in Brazil.
Save our Seas	2010	Commercial fishing ban in British territories in Indian Ocean.	221,000 signatures from 223 countries.	UK government announces twofold increase of protected marine areas.
Ficha Limpa	2011	Passage of anti-corruption legislation (*Ficha Limpa*) in the Supreme Court in Brazil.	250,000 signatures for petition submitted to President Dilma.	New Anti-Corruption legislation, *Ficha Limpa* legislation passed.
Palestine	2011	Appeal for recognition of the state of Palestine.	900,000 signatures.	Continued presence of the Palestine debate at EU level.
Stop eviction of Wall street	2011	Collection of 1 million signatures for the campaign.	800,000 signatures.	Campaign finished.

Source: Gazeta do povo 2010 and authors' compilation

Cross-sector collaboration and connected innovation

This section examines Avaaz in the context of other online petition-making platforms, highlights the differences and similarities of their approach with other initiatives and explores the relationships between this growing community and other civil society organisations, as well as other key sectors such as the media.

What makes Avaaz different?

The key difference between Avaaz and other online petition groups is its global focus. Rather than operating from national chapters or offices, as is the case with many large international NGOs, Avaaz set out to be a genuinely global organisation. The online petition-making model had already been trialled both in the US and Australia. However, in 2007, when Avaaz was founded, no one had taken the concept to a global level. This approach was chosen by the founders in recognition of the increasingly connected world in which we live, as well as the converging crises and challenges we face, such as climate change, the economic crisis decried by the indignados and Occupy Wall Street movements and political turmoil such as the Arab Spring.

> «We speak to that part of human beings' identity and that need in political campaigning to be global, as so many decisions are not made at the global level when they should be. (...) Corporations have globalised very effectively but democracies and civil society haven't.»
> —**Ricken Patel**[22]

Table 7. The world's largest online petition-making organisations

PLATFORM NAME	TARGET	MEMBERSHIP	LAUNCH	BUSINESS MODEL
Avaaz	Global	20 million	2007	Non-profit
Change	Global	*"Millions sign 1,000s of petitions each month"*	2007	For-profit
Move on	United States	5 million	1998	2 parts: 1) Non-profit; 2) Political Action Committee
Actuable	Spain	2 million	2008	For-profit (recently acquired by Change)
38 Degrees	United Kingdom	850,000	2009	Non-profit
Get up	Australia	590,000	2005	Non-profit

Source: Compiled by author

Avaaz has close working relationships with some of the other national petition-making platforms such as Move On, 38 Degrees and Get up. A number of campaigns have been carried out jointly, and in the case of 38 Degrees, Avaaz staff helped to set up the organisation and participate on the board. The "Save the Internet" campaign was run with Move On and, in Spain, an anti-corruption campaign was run in parallel with Actuable; Avaaz coordinated some of the content and initial deliveries to the main political parties, PSOE and PP. There is a sense that collaboration is very easy, given that their missions are very similar. However, the case of Change is different, primarily because it is a private company with a revenue model based on marketing and advertising to its members.

> «A lot of people in our sector are very hesitant about the model they embrace and are concerned that the money is not actually spent on change, rather on high salaries and other things that would not be acceptable in the non-profit sector.»
> —**Ricken Patel**

---

22 Interview with Ricken Patel, 9th December 2011.

Relationship with NGOs and civil society

Avaaz works closely with a diverse range of civil society organisations in a number of ways, often providing a global resource of supporters for locally initiated campaigns. Large-scale petitions are organised in partnership with international NGOs such as the campaign for the moratorium on GMOs in Europe which collected a million signatures and was presented to the European Commission by Avaaz together with Greenpeace. For national campaigns where there is already an existing organised movement for the issue in question, Avaaz will support that movement with complementary action, above all scaling up international support and media coverage, as was the case in the India Against Corruption movement and the Movement to Combat Electoral Corruption in Brazil. Likewise Avaaz has supported indigenous movements, helping to bring international attention to their plight.

> «95% of all campaigns have
> an element of strategic collaboration.»
> —**Luis Morago**[23]

There are numerous examples where Avaaz has provided the key leverage (the aforementioned tipping point) in a campaign that a local organisation may have been working on for years, or even decades. One example is the Brazilian Consumer Rights Organisation IDE, which had been lobbying the Brazilian Telecommunications Agency for regulation of internet quality for some time. Forty-eight hours before the board was finally to vote on the proposed regulation, Avaaz and IDE sent 70,000 messages directly to the board members – the regulation was immediately approved.

Where there is no organised movement, rather a feeling of discontent, as was the case for the People against Murdoch campaign, a different approach may be taken: for example, two major opinion polls were carried out by the Avaaz team to demonstrate the widespread opposition to Murdoch's acquisition plans.

Avaaz and the media

Avaaz's relationship with the media is of great significance and multifaceted. Avaaz has a network of thousands of journalists across the world, a potential source of strength which is deployed in a number of ways. On the one hand, Avaaz's role is to bring international media attention to a particular issue and help scale up international support for that issue. Alternatively, the media is used as a vehicle to directly influence the decision-makers being targeted at a key point in time. A mechanism that has been used frequently is that of buying high-impact press or TV advertisements to be published at crucial moments in international negotiating arenas.

In the case of campaigns for Burma, Tibet and the Arab Spring, the relationship with the media has been slightly different – here Avaaz's role has been to enable citizens' voices to be heard in a context of extreme media censorship. Avaaz claims that the BBC, CNN and Al Jazeera reported that at one point 40% of the images that were used in their coverage of the Arab Spring were generated by the Avaaz-supported citizens' journalist network.

---

23 Interview with Campaign Director Luis Morago, 7th November 2011.

Figure 5. Avaaz Love China campaign

Avaaz's "Love China" walking-ads at a London screening of the Beijing Olympics opening ceremony in 2008.

Finally, Avaaz has a specific line of campaigning which aims to create a more democratic media sector. In particular, it has targeted the Murdoch empire in the UK, Canada and Australia, Berlusconi's censorship proposals and, most recently, two controversial pieces of legislation: the US government bill known as the Stop Online Piracy Act (SOPA) and the international Anti-Counterfeiting Trade Agreement (ACTA). The relationship Avaaz has with the media is mutually beneficial: Avaaz benefits from coverage to scale up the impact of its campaigns, and the media benefits from Avaaz's support to help get reports from the front line in zones of major censorship.

Economic sustainability and long-term viability

Avaaz is 100% funded by small, online donations from its 20 million members around the world and has raised over $20 million online with an average donation amount of $35/€25 since 2007. Since 2010, Avaaz has not accepted any money from governments or corporations and no single donation has been more than $5,000. This section presents the core elements of Avaaz's funding strategy, describes how the financial model has changed over time and how it is projected to develop over the next 20 years.

Avaaz in numbers

Avaaz is registered as a non-profit 501 (c) 4 organisation in the state of Delaware, USA, and in compliance with US Federal Law it conducts an annual independent audit of its finances, which is made available on its website. Avaaz is required to declare and account for its expenditures in each of the following three categories: management and general expenses, programmes (i.e. campaigns), and fundraising, as shown in the graph below.

Figure 6. Avaaz's expenses from 2007 to 2010

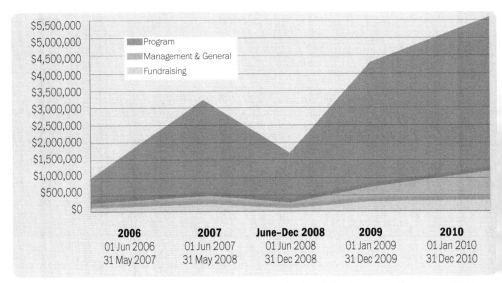

Figure 6 shows that programmes account for the majority of expenses, with an average of 82% being spent since 2007. An average of 13% has been spent on "Management & General" and 4% on "Fundraising" over the same period. Source: www.avaaz.org, accessed 25th February 2012.

Independent and accountable

In 2009, Avaaz changed its financing model by not accepting a single donation above $5,000. This has enabled the organisation to project an image of total independence. In addition the decision was made for the donations not to be tax-deductible which means the only group to be held accountable to are the members and funders of the organisation. Most crucially this also means the organisation can get involved in political lobbying campaigns.

A flat and flexible organisational structure has been set up, whereby the team is organised into smaller autonomous teams for each campaign, and this means that overheads have been kept to a minimum. The teams are selected based on their knowledge of the area, competencies and connections to other organisations working on the issue of concern, which means that teams will change for each campaign. This creates a vibrant, dynamic organisational culture in which individuals are constantly adapting to the needs of the campaign and new team members. It also encourages ongoing personal and professional development. The online nature of the work also means that there is very little office infrastructure and expenditure, with many of the team working from home or collective co-working spaces.

Fundraising strategy

There are three main channels for Avaaz's income: first, the regular members' donations, which account for around $400,000 per month and are received without any targeted campaign or message from Avaaz, i.e. this money comes "without even asking". To cover organisational costs every year, two or three emails are sent to all members, which usually raises around $1m and this is organised by a small fundraising team. The third income stream is for specific campaigns, where the more specific the proposal the better the result. For example, when raising funds to buy a newspaper or TV ad, the team will send a mock-up ad to members, ask for feedback and clearly communicate how the target could be achieved. For example "if 1,000 people donate just $5 each ad would be in the paper tomorrow". Similar strategies were used to purchase equipment for Syria and to organise an event for Palestine independence (Luis Morago).

The fundraising mechanisms used are similar to those of other online platforms – easily made online credit card payments. This differs from the earlier fundraising models such as that of Greenpeace, which uses postal services to recruit and contact its membership, organises fundraising events and other offline activities. Greenpeace, which bills members through the mail, organises fundraising events and other offline activity. However, many Greenpeace donators are now from older generations.

As the Avaaz figures show, very few of its resources are dedicated to fundraising; instead, efforts are channelled into achieving the organisation's mission and ensuring an efficient, effective, transparent, accountable, democratic organisation which generates significant social returns. This organisational culture or Avaaz's DNA is summed up in the "11 reasons to donate to Avaaz" published on the website.

Table 8. 11 reasons to donate to Avaaz

1	What we do works
2	An investment with permanent social change returns
3	World-class team that does outstanding work
4	No bureaucracy
5	Regularly audited and fiscally responsible
6	Pass the money on when it makes sense, and give to the best efforts
7	100% independent
8	Political (our donations are not tax-deductible, leaving us 100% free to do whatever needed to get leaders to listen)
9	We go where the greatest needs and opportunities are
10	Democratic accountability
11	No other organisation like us

Source: www.avaaz.org

Avaaz has just completed its initial five-year business plan, achieving all its set targets and has now chosen to adopt a 20-year planning cycle, based on the idea that many things will change so a long-term vision is being combined with a high degree of nimbleness and flexibility. The organisation's sustainability will be measured on key metrics such as the percentage of the population represented by members across all the different countries and the number of people willing to donate.

Innovation type

This section explores some of the secrets of Avaaz's success: in particular, the open innovation strategy it has used to obtain such a high level of membership and the social impact it sets out to achieve.

Global, multi-issue platform

The global focus combined with the multi-issue approach is core to Avaaz's success story. By not restricting the platform to a single thematic area such as climate change, human rights or corruption, or any one geographical focus such as Tibet, or Latin America, Avaaz has achieved a multiplier effect, whereby a member who is inspired to join Avaaz for an environmental cause may then go on to support a human rights petition, and later support a campaign for Tibet. This approach has various implications: first, the community can attract a far wider audience than a typical thematically focused NGO; second, a single member can support various causes – helping the petitions to scale quickly, and finally, when an urgent action is required, there is a large membership community to call on. In this sense, the large international NGOs who may have been working on a single issue for many years see Avaaz as a strategic resource to be mobilised for those decisive moments when action and media attention is needed.

Democratic *and* decisive

A second ingredient to Avaaz's success is the fine balance it has achieved between being, on the one hand, an open, democratic platform where members are encouraged to propose campaigns and participate in the selection process, and, on the other, having a skilled team who make an effective final selection of highlighted winnable battles that will hit all the aforementioned campaign metrics.

> «Avaaz staff don't set an agenda and try to convince members to go along with it. It's closer to the opposite: we listen to members and suggest actions they can take in order to affect the broader world.»
> —**Avaaz**[24]

In this way users are involved in the campaign selection and design process; however, the final decisions are made by a clear mission-oriented team. Recently in 2012, Avaaz launched a new Community Petitions section on its website that allows individuals and organisations to launch their own petitions.[25]

The membership engagement process includes regular surveys to assess members' feelings on the organisation's overall direction. This survey also identifies key priority areas for its members to consider and is complemented by specific surveys at crucial moments on particular campaigns or when there are

---

24 www.avaaz.org accessed 25th February 2012.

25 www.avaaz.org/en/petition

polemical issues at stake, such as religion. Besides these different surveys, Avaaz also receives dozens of proposals for campaigns from members, experts and the team every week. Of these, around 15 are discussed by the team at regular all-team teleconferences (two per week). The selected campaigns are then sent to a random sample of 10,000 or 20,000 members to gauge their reactions. Based on the responses, together with the potential impact of the campaign, timing issues, Avaaz's added value and other considerations, a decision is made on which campaigns (national, regional and global), are fully launched (Luis Morago).[26]

Clear communication

Avaaz has a wealth of communication expertise and this helps to channel members' attention to where help is most needed; deploying an accessible journalistic approach to ensure effective communication, writing email alerts "in a way that an aide briefs a prime minister", is crucial for a campaign's success when attention often has to be captured in an instant. An example of this is the use of full-page adverts in newspapers as shown in Figure 4. Other mechanisms to help ensure campaigns' focus include the absence of a search engine, which helps to limit distraction and channel traffic to the campaigns on the home page, slight variations for the different language versions of national campaigns and the regularly updated petition targets to maintain the image of "we're nearly there, with your help we could make it".

Figure 7. Avaaz campaign against the criminalisation of emergency birth control

An example of a recent Avaaz campaign. A 682,790-signature petition being handed over to politicians in Honduras to stop the criminalisation of women's emergency birth control. After the petition was delivered, the MPs agreed to set up meetings with local groups to define a strategy to stop the law.

26 Interview with Campaign Director Luis Morago, 7th November 2011.

Scalability and replicability

The Avaaz community has witnessed an exponential growth over the last five years, both in membership and in individual donations. Continuing to scale up its activity with excellence has been identified as a core challenge for Avaaz and this section describes why and how the organisation expects to grow in the next 20 years.

Projected growth

In 2011, the organisation came to the end of its first five-year business plan, having achieved all its aims and targets. It is now embarking on a 20-year planning cycle based on the idea that many things will change, but that the ability to act fast must continue. Although the plan is currently being drawn up, it will include ambitious targets to draw specific percentages of the population of different countries into membership; this will build on the 1–2% already achieved in some countries. Avaaz is also studying organisational models not typically followed by civil society organisations – such as Apple and Walmart. Avaaz is already the largest web movement in history and continues to grow at a striking rate (in January 2012, one and a half million people signed up), and thus its potential to influence politics and opinion at a global level is completely unprecedented.

There is overwhelming support from users for Avaaz to expand its team so that it can have a still greater impact. In the 2012 New Year's users' survey, 74% supported the growth of Avaaz's team, 25% were not sure and only 2% disagreed with the proposal.

Management challenges

For the first few years of its existence, Avaaz was a small team of 15 people operating mostly online from different countries. In 2009, the team grew from 30 to 80 for a temporary climate change campaign, which was considered a successful experiment in scaling up with excellence; *we found we could ingrain the culture if we chose the right people,* stated Ricken Patel. Until 2011, Avaaz was organised into three tiers: executive director, campaign directors and campaigners. In late 2011, a further 40 staff were hired. Avaaz currently has 80 staff members and has recently shifted to a five-layer structure (executive director, campaigns manager, campaign director, senior campaigners and campaigners), based on a ratio of 15 staff for every campaign manager. The campaign teams are kept deliberately small (2 to 5 people) and individuals are constantly moved around so the development of silos is avoided and everyone is able to speak on behalf of the organisation as a whole regarding the decisions they have to make. There is a conscious focus on developing a slick organisational culture based on the most effective delivery of campaigns possible.

> «I didn't get my inspiration at Walmart, but I got some confirmation about a management approach: organisational culture is key.»
> —**Ricken Patel**[27]

---

27 Interview with Ricken Patel, 9th December 2011.

Global reach challenges

Finally, a challenge to further scaling up of Avaaz's activity is the need to make the website available in more languages: overcoming translation barriers, teams of people are required to translate the material into multiple languages and communicate in a clear language that resonates with the cultures being targeted. Currently efforts are being made to translate into Arabic, Japanese, Russian, Korean and Hindi. Finally, maintaining the global vision, whereby campaigns resonate with people from countries all around the world, is a continuing challenge which requires a fast analysis and selection process. As the community grows and the campaign proposals multiply, this will become a still greater challenge.

———

Appendix 1. Selection of press campaigns

The following appendix shows examples of Avaaz's full-page adverts to support key campaigns.

Advertisement featured in the Financial Times on 9th December 2011, at the time of the COP17 Climate talks in Durban. The advertisement addresses India, Japan, the US and Canada; and its powerful message caused some consternation even among other activists.

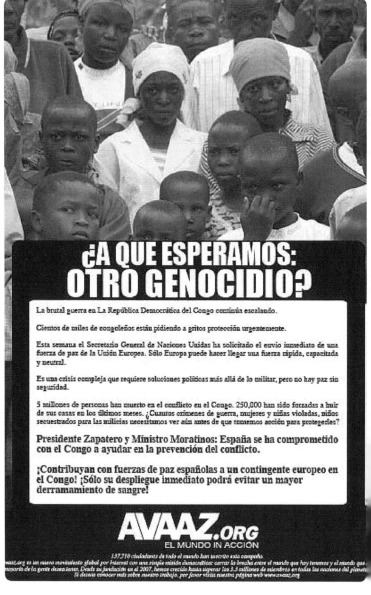

Avaaz's advertisement for its Republic of Congo campaign published in El País *in 2008 to support the deployment of Spanish peacekeepers to the country to stop further bloodshed.*
Photo: Laura Rico Piñeres

———

Appendix 2. Users' survey 2012

154,378 people from 195 countries, in 9 different languages, took part in the survey at the end of 2011 and identified the following as the priority issues for Avaaz to focus on in 2012.

PRIORITY ISSUE	% OF VOTES
Human rights	77.32%
Economic policy for the public good	68.12%
Political corruption	67.68%
Climate change and the environment	67.,68%

PRIORITY ISSUE	% OF VOTES
Democracy movements	59.90%
War and peace	62.44%
Poverty and development	61.34%
Food and health	49.56%
Biodiversity and conservation	54.29%

Based on a selection of Avaaz's campaigns, users prioritised the following issues.

PRIORITY ISSUE	% OF VOTES
Fight the "rape trade"	63.43%
Support movements such as Occupy Wall Street or Indignados and challenge the influence of corporations in our democracies	62.19%
Stop deforestation	66.62%
Stop political corruption	61.27%
Achieve a strong global climate treaty	60.75%
Regulate agribusiness and the food industry	50.02%
Global disarmament	53.88%
Help end poverty	48.03%
Promote peace in Israel–Palestine	46.63%
Protect internet freedom	50.55%

PRIORITY ISSUE	% OF VOTES
Protect our oceans and biodiversity	56.94%
Protect free media	49.50%
Protect freedom of information	51.48%
End fossil fuel subsidies	50.73%
Stop anti-gay laws	37.48%
Pressure China to play a more responsible international role and end repression in Tibet	43.86%
Support the Arab Spring movements	32.90%
End the war on drugs	32.80%

———

References

Avaaz

www.avaaz.org. Accessed between December 2011 and February 2012.

El País

Avaaz Republic of Congo campaign advertisement published in 2008.

Financial Times

"Will they sign Africa's death sentence?" Advertisement published 9th December 2011.

Gazeta do povo

"Website mobilises 10 million for collective action", published 30th October 2010.

Luis Morago

Campaign Director for Avaaz, interviewed 7th November 2011.

New York Times (2008)

"Richest nations pledge to half greenhouse gases", published 9th July 2008.

Ricken Patel

Chief Executive of Avaaz, interviewed 9th December 2011.

***Time* magazine** (2012)

"How a New York City based activist has become a player in Syria," published 15th March 2012.

Times of India (2011)

"Indian origin Canadian is voice of Jan Lokpal", published 11th August 2011.

Barcelona Food Bank: the *"Big Food Collection"* campaign

«In 2011 the Big Food Collection collected 1,100 tons of food (equivalent to €2m). What single NGO can raise two million euros in a day? It's simple – the Big Food Collection works because people know the food goes to the poor. From a commercial perspective the message is clear.»
—**Jordi Peix,** Founder of Barcelona Food Bank

Mission	Fight poverty and food waste, with a yearly "Big Food Collection" campaign to raise awareness of both issues.
Founded	The Foundation was launched in 1987 and the first "Big Food Collection" in 2009.
Scalability	Currently works at a regional level and is helping other cities to replicate the campaign with potential to scale to national level.
Location	Barcelona, Spain
Financing	Donations from the food industry, public administration, businesses and individuals.
Social impact	In 2011, more than 180 towns participated with 600 collection points, 7,600 volunteers and a total of 1,100 tonnes of food collected and distributed.
Open innovation	Yes, a shared concept across Europe.
Innovation	An effective, low-cost, solidarity food chain that responds to gaps between demand and supply.

Introduction

This section gives an overview of the Barcelona Food Bank as an organisation, what it set out to achieve, its founding principles and how it functions over the course of a year. We then introduce the Bank's major campaign, the "Big Food Collection" (*La Gran Recapte* in Catalan) and the role it plays in helping to achieve the organisation's overall mission.

The Barcelona Food Bank (*Fundació Banc d'Aliments* in Catalan), was founded as a non-profit Foundation in 1987 by Jordi Peix, the then Director General of the Catalan Government's Department of Agriculture and Fisheries. Jordi was inspired on one hand by Brazilian activist Josué de Castro's[28] work on urban poverty and, on the other, the Food Bank models already operating in various European countries. The Foundation was financed with private funds from the founder and a small group of colleagues and it set out to achieve two clear parallel objectives: fight poverty and hunger in the Barcelona area and reduce food wastage.

---

28 Josúe de Castro, a Brazilian nutritionist, activist and former chairman of the World Food Organisation, is best known for his book *The Geography of Hunger*, published in 1946.

Founding principles

The Barcelona Food Bank operates under two clear principles; the first is that it is free: "nothing is bought and nothing is sold" (Antoni Sansalvadó, President of Barcelona Food Bank).[29] Food enters the bank free and is distributed to those who need it most, for free. Where possible all donations are made in the form of food instead of money, and on no account is the food distributed ever sold to the final recipient. The second principle is volunteerism. The bank was founded by a group of volunteers, who at the outset advertised for a volunteer director general and only 14 years later, in 2000, did the Bank begin to use paid staff. Today, the Barcelona Food Bank has 7 full-time paid staff and a team of 121 volunteers who work an average of 12 hours per week.

Barcelona Food Bank works in a context of increasing poverty; in Spain unemployment has risen from 9% to 20% in the last four years. The same period has witnessed extremely high levels of food wastage. According to the Agència de Residus de Catalunya, on average 7% of all solid food purchased is wasted every year in Catalonia with a value of €841m; this is equivalent to the amount needed to feed 500,000 people for an entire year, or comparable to not using 234,022 hectares of agricultural land.[30]

> «The greatest scandal is not that people go hungry, but that food is wasted. The food industry wastes food, institutions waste food, companies waste food, households waste food and at the same time people go hungry.»
> —**Jordi Peix**, Founder of Barcelona Food Bank

Solidarity food chain

Barcelona Food Bank has created an innovative food chain between donor companies who give food, recipient organisations who distribute food to individuals in high-risk economic situations and volunteers committed to fight poverty and waste. In 2011, this network comprised 320 donor companies, 311 recipient organisations and 200 volunteers cooperating throughout the year to help 114,845 individuals in need. The system, known as a solidarity food chain, is based on the identification of gaps between food demand and food supply. Once surplus food is located, it is collected, classified in the Bank's warehouses and delivered to those in need with a set of regulations applied to ensure that the food meets all sanitary requirements once it reaches its final destination. Food is delivered from donors on a weekly basis and each recipient organisation visits the Bank at least once a month to collect their share which is calculated according to the number and type of people they serve (e.g. old people, undernourished children, the terminally ill, participants on drug rehabilitation programmes, etc.).

---

29 Interview with Antoni Sansalvadó, President of Barcelona Food Bank, 14th March 2012.

30 According to the *Agència de Residus de Catalunya*, 262,471 tons of food are wasted every year in Catalonia by the food retail industry, restaurants and bars and domestic households, which is equivalent to 34.9 kg per person per year or 96 grams per person per day.

Figure 8. Barcelona Food Bank's Human Solidarity Chain

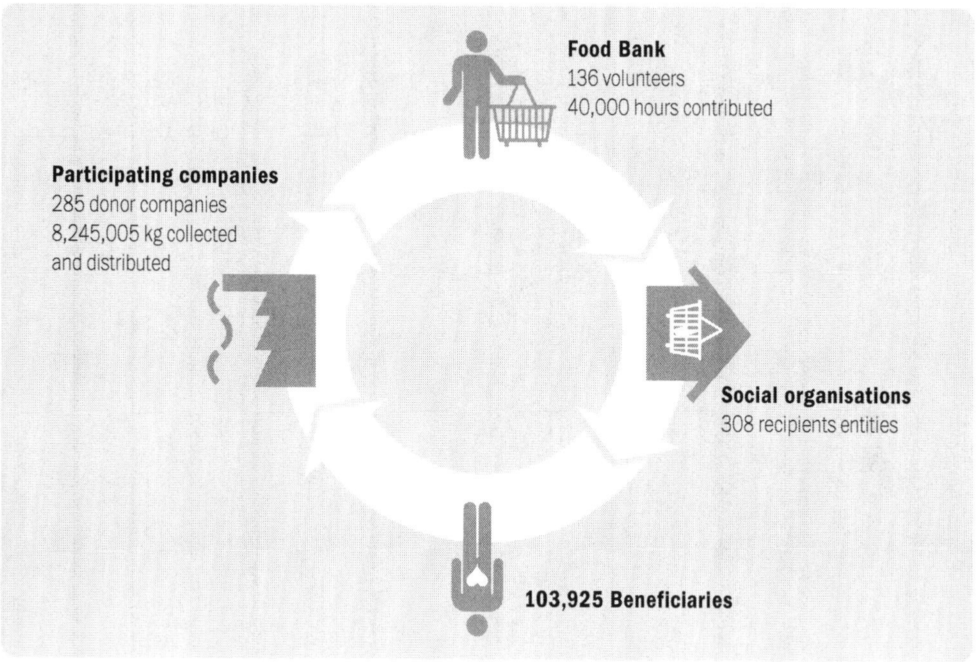

Food Bank
136 volunteers
40,000 hours contributed

Participating companies
285 donor companies
8,245,005 kg collected
and distributed

Social organisations
308 recipients entities

103,925 Beneficiaries

Source: Barcelona Food Bank Annual Report 2010

The Big Food Collection Campaign

In order to achieve its core objectives of fighting poverty and eliminating food waste, the Barcelona Food Bank has a third objective which is to foster solidarity regarding poverty and hunger and this is largely achieved through its annual campaign, the "Big Food Collection". In collaboration with the three other food banks in Catalonia, individuals and organisations donate food at a series of collection points in supermarkets, schools and other public places. The food is then delivered to the four food banks, classified and redistributed to recipient organisations across Catalonia. The campaign runs over the course of three days in November. Following two days of collecting (Friday and Saturday) and one day of classifying (Sunday), the food is ready to be distributed the following Monday. The first Big Food Collection was organised in 2009. In 2011 more than 180 towns and 7,600 volunteers participated in the campaign, during which a total of 1,095 tons of food was collected from 600 collection points (300 of which are in Barcelona) and then distributed to organisations across Catalonia. The Big Food Collection is targeted at the general public as well as the food industry and, in 2010, an online donation system was introduced to increase public participation in the campaign by enabling those people who were unable to reach a collection point to make online food or cash donations. The food donated during the campaign amounts to around 10% of the food collected annually and is valued at €2m.

Figure 9. Collection point at Caprabo Supermarket in Barcelona

Achievements so far

This section gives a brief history of what the organisation has achieved since it was founded 25 years ago and goes on to trace the evolution of the Big Food Collection since the campaign was first adopted in 2009. While the organisation has shown steady growth since it was founded, the introduction of the Big Food Collection in 2009 marked a significant step in its history. It is worthy of note that these achievements have been made by a team of only seven salaried staff (the first of whom was hired in 2000) and an increasing group of volunteers.

25 years of fighting poverty

The Barcelona Food Bank has shown continued growth since it was founded in 1987 in terms of its results (measured in kilos of food collected and the number of beneficiaries) and its organisation (calculated according to the numbers of donating organisations, recipient organisations and volunteers). Two key moments in the organisation's history were: first, the employment of a salaried director in 2000; and, second, the organisation of the first Big Food Collection in 2009.

Table 9. Barcelona Food Bank's history in five phases

	PHASE 1		PHASE 2		PHASE 3		PHASE 4	PHASE 5	
ADDRESS	BOFARULL, 11		PG TORRAS I BAGES, 154		SARDENYA, 372		MOTORS, 122 (RENOVATION)	MOTORS, 122	
YEAR	**1988**	**1997**	**1998**	**2000**	**2001**	**2003**	**2004**	**2004**	**2010**
Tons of food	227	1,026	1,251	2,050	2,084	2,138	1,869	7,402	8,245
Donating organisations	29	132	161	201	240	332	340	402	285
Recipient organisations	64	237	253	244	246	275	281	296	308
Volunteers	18	36	36	41	45	56	57	89	136
Beneficiaries	1,500	44,000	44,000	47,000	48,000	55,525	57,000	91,862	10,925
Value of food (million €)	0.4	2.57	3.11	4.83	5.45	5.28	4.67	15.6	19

Source: Barcelona Food Bank Annual Report 2011

The proportion of food income from local donations increased significantly from 34% to 48% of the total donations when the first Big Food Collection was organised in 2009. While its percentage contribution has continued at this level since then, the number of donations has been increasing and has even risen above the EU contribution.

Table 10. Barcelona Food Bank income (2008–2012)

	2008	**2009**	**2010**	**2011**	**2012** (estimated)
Total (tons)	7,043	7,402	8,245	10,161	14,000
EU donations	4,630	3,847	3,751	4,746	7,500
Donations and collections	2,413	3,554	4,493	5,465	6,500
% of total	34%	48%	51%	54%	46%
Beneficiaries	57,381	79,899	103,925	115,129	120,000
Recipient organisations	279	282	308	310	312
kg/beneficiary	122.7	92.6	79.3	88.3	116.6

Source: Barcelona Food Bank Annual Report 2011

The food donated to the Barcelona Food Bank comes from a range of sources, the largest of which is the European Union, which distributes excess food from international markets to each European country in proportion to its population and gross domestic product. The second-largest donor to Barcelona, the second-largest city in Spain and a major European port, is the food industry itself. The Barcelona Food Bank has ongoing agreements with ten large food distribution companies, six of which deliver food once a week. The Barcelona Food Bank goes to the warehouses of the remaining four, to collect their contributions on a weekly basis. Another major source of food income is the agricultural sector, which makes contributions mostly on the basis of seasonal fluctuations in production, and miscalculations of supply and demand.

Table 11. Barcelona Food Bank food income breakdown for 2011

SECTOR	TONS	% OF TOTAL	
Food industry	2,555	25%	
Distribution sector	650	6%	Markets (481 tons) Supermarkets (167 tons)
Donations and *Big Food Collection*	1,005	10%	
Agricultural production	1,170	12%	Fruit juice (422 tons) Fruit (750 tons)
European Union	4,750	47%	
Total	10,169	100%	

Source: Barcelona Food Bank Annual Report 2011

25 years of reducing waste

Every year the Barcelona Food Bank prevents millions of kilos of food that has been classified as "edible but not commercial" from being wasted. This is achieved by identifying key entry points in the food chain which include the following:

Proximity to sell-by date: supermarkets will only stock food on their shelves which has a specific sell-by date, use-by date or best-before date. Once this is reduced to a week or less the company is likely to take the food off the shelves and either destroy it (costing money), dispose of it in landfill (which is illegal), or give it to a food bank. Barcelona Food Bank often receives food with only seven days left on its shelf-life meaning it needs a quick turnaround to reach the final consumer.

Over-production: Spain has a high level of agricultural production, and due to the latent 5% error in the agricultural sector's supply and demand calculations, at certain times of year there is a production surplus. Barcelona Food Bank manages over-production by converting fruit into juice and fruit preserves or simply redistributing fruit and vegetables that can no longer be sold in traditional retail outlets to recipient organisations.

Production imperfections: often companies will not sell products that have a minor visual imperfection, such as the surface texture of a pâté. In these cases, Barcelona Food Bank accepts the product for redistribution.

Seasonal fluxes: due to the lack of perfection in production calculations often companies cannot sell products beyond their seasonal demand (e.g. Panettone after Christmas, Gazpacho after the sum mer). These fluxes can also occur on a daily basis, on a particularly hot day, more ice-cream and less yoghurt will be sold and, as a result, more yoghurt (with a shorter shelf-life than ice-cream) nears its sell-by date.

Public recognition

The Barcelona Food Bank is now almost as well known across Spain as one of the country's largest and most recognised NGOs, Intermón, which is the Spanish branch of Oxfam. A study carried out in 2011 compared the Barcelona Food Bank's reputation to that of Intermón and the Spanish branch of Médecins sans Frontières.[31] Across Spain, 55% of the population had heard of the Barcelona Food Bank (only seven points below Intermón). While over half of the participants had heard of the Barcelona Food Bank only 17% knew exactly what the organisation did; a large majority believed that it sent food to developing countries or raised money to buy food for the poor. On the whole, the Barcelona Food Bank is better known among people aged between 35 and 49 from middle-class groups and there is a greater recognition and understanding of its activity in the Barcelona metropolitan area.

Figure 10. Food being delivered to the Barcelona Food Bank

Impact and degree of transformation

What is the real impact of the Big Food Collection and to what extent does it help the Barcelona Food Bank achieve its mission? How has it helped to fight poverty and reduce food wastage in Catalonia? This section describes the degree of transformation that the Big Food Collection has achieved not only in terms of the kilos of food donated, but above all in how the mobilisation of civil society to address local poverty has

---

31 The study was based on telephone interviews with 1,000 people aged between 15 and 75 from different socio-economic groups. It was carried out pro bono by the market research company TNS: www.tnsglobal.es.

repercussions throughout the year for the Barcelona Food Bank's operations. The impact of the Big Food Collection is clear; since it began it has been growing exponentially, both in terms of the kilos collected and the numbers of volunteers participating, which reached an impressive 7,600 in 2011.

Table 12. Growth figures for the Barcelona Food Bank's Big Food Collection since 2009

	2009	2010	2011
Number of volunteers	200	3,800	7,600
Kilos collected	200,000 kg	400,000 kg	1,127,000 kg
% of total kg	2.7%	10.5%	14.8%

Source: Barcelona Food Bank

Visibility and publicity

Before starting the Big Food Collection, the Barcelona Food Bank team went to visit the Portuguese Food Bank to learn from their experience and it also consulted projects being run in France and Italy. The first impression was that the Big Food Collection was an excellent mechanism to collect more kilos of food. However, the Barcelona team also learned that the food is just one part of the campaign's results, and that the publicity the campaign generates leads to a far greater impact.

The three-day campaign is organised by a communications team of 20 people over a period of six months, and although the food collected does make a significant contribution to the work of the Barcelona Food Bank (amounting to roughly what the Bank collects over the course of a typical month), the greatest impact of the Big Food Collection is the publicity it generates for the organisation, which has positive repercussions for the rest of the year. The Big Food Collection gets the Barcelona Food Bank into the news, shows it in action at street level, and introduces its activities to people's daily lives.

Much of the campaign's success is due to a clear communication strategy based on a high degree of visibility. With teams of volunteers wearing Big Food Collection T-shirts at supermarket checkouts manning large Big Food Collection boxes full of food, there is an extremely high probability that passing customers will put something in the food box. Multiply this experience 600 times across Catalonia for two days and it is clear how the campaign also attracts media attention.

In 2011, the Big Food Collection campaign featured on the front page of the national newspaper, *La Vanguardia* for three days in a row. It was also highlighted on the TV station TV3, COMRàdio and numerous other Catalan media organisations. The Barcelona Food Bank Team agree that the Big Food Collection helps them achieve their goal throughout the year by generating good publicity that serves to boost donations and support from businesses, the food industry and individuals for the rest of the year.

There are two sides to the relationship with the press; firstly, there is the offer of free publicity and adverts, but this is not nearly as useful as the second aspect, which is the personal commitment from individual journalists, who by writing an article, including an interview on the radio or even publishing news about the campaign on their front pages can have much more impact. This personal relationship with journalists and media representatives inspired by the campaign is central to the visibility achieved by the Big Food Collection. The relationship with the public sector is similar to that with the press as it gives the campaign credibility and visibility. For example, the mayor of Barcelona might participate in a promotional activity for the campaign, as will political representatives from smaller towns across Catalonia.

> «On the day of the Big Food Collection you collect food,
> and for the rest of the year you harvest the real fruit of your labour.»
> —**Antoni Sansalvadó,** President of the Barcelona Food Bank

> «You spend six months organising a campaign and right after it's over its benefits come in: a whole series of schools, businesses and volunteers approach you after the campaign, offering to help, donate money, organise a campaign and so on. The response is incredible and we can barely keep up responding to the offers to help.»
> —**Laia Guinjoan,** Director of Communications

One example of the kind of help offered is that of an IT company SAP, which came to Barcelona to organise a conference. Having heard about the Barcelona Food Bank through the Big Food Collection campaign, the company organised its own campaign where participants had to bring a kilo of rice to the conference. In addition to the rice collected at the conference, the company also donated €40,000 and offered to install a new software system for the organisation.

Stimulating latent solidarity

The number of volunteers involved in the Big Food Collection has grown exponentially since its first year in 2009. According to the organisation's President the secret of this success is that the Big Food Collection offers a practical way to help others in need. He considers this as key to mobilising support not just for food donating organisations, but for all kinds of civil society organisations.

> «At the end of the day people don't need much persuading to do good,
> they just need a good enough reason and a practical solution.»
> —**Antoni Sansalvadó**[32]

Recognising that there is a latent sense of solidarity in us all, the Big Food Collection provides an opportunity for individuals to easily make a contribution to those less well off than themselves; what could be easier and more immediate than adding an extra food item to your shopping trolley in order to donate to a group of people with smiling faces at the checkout? In 2011, journalists posed the question to Barcelona Food Bank, "*What about the crisis? How will you manage?*" and, surprisingly, the response has been greater than ever. In the President's view, this may perhaps be precisely because so many people know someone close to them who is in economic difficulty or unemployed and so they are even more inclined to help; "*Yes, we have been in crisis, but more people have come and with their pockets fuller than ever*" (Antoni Sansalvadó).

Another motivation for getting involved in the Big Food Collection is the atmosphere created on the day that the donations are classified. In 2010, managers from Kraft Foods, the second-largest food multinational,

---

32 Interview with Antoni Sansalvadó, President of Barcelona Food Bank, 14th March 2012.

were so inspired by the classification day's buzz of activity and the fraternal spirit of the thousands of volunteers classifying tons of kilos of food accompanied by music blasted through the warehouse that they decided to send 30 members of their senior management team to participate the following year.

Addressing the nutritional imbalance

In addition to the publicity generated and the stimulus provided for individuals to volunteer their time and money another important impact of the Big Food Collection is the nutritional balance it provides for beneficiaries. During the course of the year the Barcelona Food Bank does not accept eggs, fish or meat, as this would require a logistical and refrigeration infrastructure that would make the operation unsustainable. As a result of this, the balance between lipids, glucids and proteins is not always met during the year so specific products are requested during the Big Food Collection: for example, high-protein products such as tins of tuna. As these products have a relatively long shelf-life and are more expensive than the typically donated rice and pasta, fewer donations of them are made throughout the year. Jars of legumes (lentils, chick peas and beans), olive oil, which does not expire and is also a high-value product, are also rarely donated throughout the year, so again for their nutritional value they are requested on the days of the Big Food Collection. The Big Food Collection focuses on the quality rather than the quantity of food to address the nutritional imbalance affecting the impoverished groups targeted.

Figure 11. Big Food Collection poster, 2011

Cross-sector collaboration and connected innovation

This section examines the Barcelona Food Bank's relationships with its core stakeholders – the food industry, other donor organisations and the recipient organisations – and considers how they ensure it meets its overall objectives. We also discuss how these relationships ensure that the Big Food Collection campaign has the desired impact all year round.

The food industry

According to the President of the Barcelona Food Bank, mass-produced manufactured foodstuffs that go unsold often end up in landfill sites. Besides incurring high economic costs, this practice can cause environmental contamination if not processed correctly because some foods do not decompose naturally and others such as dairy products can cause harm to water sources. Other products end up on what are known as semi-legal secondary markets and are sold on a commission basis. A food bank typically diverts products from going to waste or being resold on the black market, classifies them, and thanks to an efficient network of organisations ensures the food's rapid distribution to those in need.

The message to the food industry is that, by donating food to the Barcelona Food Bank, companies can avoid not only the financial costs of disposing of food, such as payment of a landfill tax (although currently in Spain this is still an insignificant sum unlike other countries such as the UK where it is much more prohibitive), but also the intangible of costs of the bad press associated with selling on their products through the black market for food. As a result they can gain credibility and transparency. In addition to the intangible gains, a 35% tax reduction is applicable to all donations.

There are three types of food company that work with the Barcelona Food Bank. First, those that deliver food to the Bank on a regular, weekly basis as part of their distribution process (this is the case with a number of large companies – Danone, Grupo Leche Pascual, Kraft Foods Spain, Unilever Foods Spain and Wrigley. A second group donates regularly but they do not deliver the products to the food bank. Finally, a third group donates sporadically when they have a surplus for a variety of reasons, which could be seasonal over-production or an unforeseen occurrence such as a transport strike which means they cannot deliver their product to its intended destination. The Barcelona Food Bank's relationship with the food industry is changing as companies are becoming more efficient and thus wasting less food. As a result the Bank has engaged with more companies, and now has relationships with a series of smaller companies who donate sporadically.

For the purposes of the Big Food Collection, two people from the fundraising department who manage the relationships with the 20 to 30 regular donor companies throughout the year call each company individually to ask for their support during the campaign, by donating specific products, collaborating with transport provision, hosting a collection point or sending staff as volunteers.

The non-food sector industry

In line with its fundamental principles and so as not to confuse its core message, the Barcelona Food Bank generally asks for food rather than monetary donations, and this is also the case with companies from outside the food sector. In 2010, 52 solidarity collections were organised in non-food-sector companies. For example, Endesa, the energy company, for its centenary celebration organised a series of concerts with a Brazilian band and set a kilo of rice for the Barcelona Food Bank as the entrance fee. Other companies offered logistical help, donated vehicles and in some cases made cash donations. Companies who collaborated in this way include Credit Suisse, Fundación Prevent, Gas Natural, Invitrogen, Volkswagen and Endesa. For the communications team the message is simple and it is relatively straightforward to secure a donation, as Laia Guinjoan, Director of Communications, stated: "*It is a closed circle of human solidarity: companies are interested in helping the Food Bank because the Food Bank helps others; the message is clear.*"[33]

The Barcelona Food Bank has a number of basic operational costs and during the year the fundraising team seeks out companies to help cover these costs. Wherever possible, donations are asked only for specific items, such as a new vehicle, or an installation at the warehouse or a piece of software. The team also tries to identify companies outside the food sector with corporate social responsibility programmes, through which groups of volunteers carry out projects such as building maintenance, food classification or even organising their own company food collections. The most effective way of convincing these organisations to take part is by inviting them to the warehouse to see the operations. "*Once they see that this is not a shack, but rather a well-run business they are immediately impressed,*" said the organisation's President Antoni Sansalvadó. While the Big Food Collection is under way, these companies are approached again to give extra support during the campaign.

Recipient organisations

The next stage in this food chain is the recipient organisations which include institutions such as old people's homes, shelter providers for homeless people, immigrants' support centres, orphanages and rehabilitation centres. Relationships with these organisations are carefully managed throughout the year and require special attention during the Big Food Collection campaign. As with all of the elements of this solidarity food chain, the network of recipient organisations has grown enormously since the campaign began. From initially reaching 7,000 people in 2008, the Barcelona Food Bank now has 120,000 beneficiaries. According to the President, when the network was smaller, everyone knew each other well and the recipient organisations did not ask for much. Now that both the network and the Bank's capacity and reputation have grown, the relationships are more complex with recipient organisations asking for additional support beyond food donations, especially regarding volunteering for major food collections such as the Big Food Collection or Operación Kilo run by the Carrefour and Eroski supermarket chains.

As the network has grown, so have the risks of the system being abused, and there is now a monitoring system in place to ensure that the recipient organisations do not go against the philosophy of the Bank by selling on the food they receive. In a recent case an organisation was discovered selling the food donated to it by Barcelona Food Bank. The organisation in question was removed from the network. In another case, an old people's home was also removed, as the Barcelona Food Bank considered it was abusing the system because it was already receiving support from public authorities to cover food costs. Monitoring is organised through an annual survey, as well as a minimum of at least one visit to the organisation every year. In addition, meetings are organised to bring the different entities together. This was previously organised according to the type of entity; however, more recently geographical location has been adopted as the criterion, which has enabled a host of practical collaborations, such as sharing transport or storage space and sharing resources for the Big Food Collection. Sustained contact with the recipient organisations is essential for the weekly operations and for requesting additional involvement from them during the Big Food Collection.

---

33 Interview with Laia Guinjoan, Director of Communications, 14th March 2012.

During the Big Food Collection, the recipient organisations are asked to volunteer for activities at supermarkets or markets over the two days of food collecting. All the food collected is then delivered by transportation companies and via distribution chains to the Food Bank warehouse. There, all the food is sorted and then distributed according to a principle of fairness; each recipient organisation receives an amount calculated on the basis of the number and type of people it serves. Only those recipient organisations providing volunteers for collection points outside of a 50 km radius from Barcelona are able to take what is collected directly to their centres. The rest of the food collected at the volunteer collection points is transported to the Bank's warehouse. This may mean that a small organisation that feeds 20 people might collect 5,000 kg of food to deliver to Barcelona because it is located next to a large supermarket; however, it will only receive 500 kg after the sorting of the donations is completed. Likewise, a larger organisation may only collect 500 kg as it is based near a small supermarket, but it will receive a larger proportion based on the number of people it serves. The contrast between these cases illustrates the principle of fairness. This system is applied to the distribution of donations throughout the year as well as to the Big Food Collection. Coordinating this process requires a considerable amount of human resources and the ability to motivate donors and volunteers; particularly as the related organisations may not have adequate human resources for the voluntary work required of them and will in turn have to find others to help. The core message is:

> «the food we collect in this campaign will be distributed to all recipient organisations, including yours, so all we ask is for your volunteers help to collect food so we can continue helping you.»
> —**Laia Guinjoan**

For the recipient organisations that only receive donations during the Big Food Collection, the system is simpler and they are willing to collect whatever is allocated.

Other key stakeholders in the Campaign's food chain are **consumers** and **volunteers**, as well as the **other Catalan food banks** in Girona, Lleida and Reus. The latter operate in parallel with Barcelona's for the Big Food Collection. Because their resources are more limited, they draw on support from Barcelona particularly in terms of communication.

Economic sustainability and long-term viability

The Barcelona Food Bank operates according to a strict philosophy of economic sustainability, keeping operational costs to a minimum, using volunteers to carry out their work as much as they can and ensuring that food comes into the bank for free.

Operational excellence

At the core of the Barcelona Food Bank's operations is a well-managed warehouse, where food is delivered, classified according to its nutritional value, sell-by date and type of food, labelled, stored and then organised for collection by, or delivery to, the recipient. Given that much of the food that reaches the Bank has a very short shelf-life (which could be as short as seven days), the process of classification and redistribution has to happen very quickly to ensure that food is delivered within its use by date. This process is managed by the logistics and warehouse department, made up of a team of 43 volunteers. For visitors to the warehouse, the impression is of a well-run business, with conveyor belts to sort the food as it comes into the warehouse, labelled boxes and storage zones, forklift trucks and a forecourt of lorries and delivery vans. In addition, every item that enters the Bank is meticulously registered within the Bank's database.

> «Even though we are a not-for-profit organisation we must operate according to all the positive criteria businesses have, efficiency, good administration, economising wherever possible, just as a business would do.»
> **—Antoni Sansalvadó**, President

This core operational efficiency is supported by a clear management structure, with a board of 12 trustees, a management team and 19 departments, each of which is assigned a manager, has a clear set of responsibilities and is accountable to the organisation's core objectives. The departments are: administration and finance, EU food, suppliers, donations and certificates, advisory and research, communication, regional delegations, distribution and recipient organisations, schools, campaigns, logistics and warehouse, fundraising, human resources and volunteers, general secretary, food security, IT, and administration. The differences from a conventional business are that the staff are volunteers, the clients (recipient organisations) do not pay for the goods they receive and the suppliers or donor companies deliver their goods for free.

> The core operational efficiency works throughout the year, but it is put to the test over the two days of the Big Food Collection and the weeks that follow, as instead of the usual team of 43 volunteers in the warehouse there are up to 600 working in groups of as many as 80 at any one time. Furthermore, the amount received over the course of the weekend is the same as that usually received over the course of a month. The system, however, is identical to that which is used during the rest of the year: the same classification process is applied, the products are registered electronically in the same way, and the volunteers follow the same routine. However, the transport and logistics are much more complex; usually, each organisation would visit the Bank once a month to collect their share of food. Over the course of the Big Food Collection weekend, each recipient organisation may visit at least once, with extra vehicles to allow for the extra food that has to be redistributed.

Figure 12. Barcelona Food Bank warehouse

The Barcelona Food Bank warehouse has 2,535 m² of storage space, capacity for 1,300 pallets, 66 m² of refrigeration space and six vehicles (two of which are refrigerated).

Satisfied volunteers

A spirit of volunteering has been at the heart of the Barcelona Food Bank since it was founded and the organisation now has a team of 121 volunteers supporting 4,500 volunteers in the recipient organisations and a total of 7,600 volunteers who participate in the Big Food Collection.

Essential to the successful management of these volunteers is that they are rewarded for their work, not in monetary terms, but through a sense of satisfaction that they are contributing to something effective and meaningful. The rigorous measurement of how much food is delivered and how many people benefit is one element of ensuring the volunteers get this sense of satisfaction, but being part of an effective, well-organised operation is also important. The volunteers often visit the recipient organisations and this creates an emotional bond with their work; however, according to the founder it is not "*visiting the poor*" that makes you feel good, but rather "*doing a job well that you know is useful*". Attention to this issue is important and a lot of communication is devoted to ensuring that this objective is achieved.

For the Big Food Collection, this underlying philosophy is maintained, and scaled up to a wholly different dimension. The volunteers are coordinated in this case not by the volunteers department but by the communications department, usually a team of 16 people, but for the Big Food Collection a team of 20. For the first Big Food Collection in 2009, the team launched a campaign to call on individuals to volunteer, with a total of 200 volunteers participating; however, by the second year, the team quickly realised that it would be far more effective to ask groups of people to volunteer, and so began to target Scouts associations, schools, sports clubs and any other kind of group they could find. The response was extremely positive and the number of volunteers grew by more than tenfold to 3,800. The team also learned that managing the volunteers in teams was far more effective than managing them individually and so would ask for a volunteer coordinator for each group and for each collection point. This meant that they had only to deal with around 300 people to distribute campaign materials (boxes, T-shirts, posters) rather than the whole 7,600. For example, to manage the 39 markets in Barcelona the Communications team simply called a particularly well-established group of volunteers (Voluntarios 2000) who took on the whole process. Over time, the volunteer coordinators also develop a sense of satisfaction and, year upon year, go on to manage more volunteers and organise more collection points.

Diversity of income

Another important aspect of the economic sustainability of the Barcelona Food Bank is the increasing diversity of its income, both in food and monetary terms. In the early phases of its existence, the Bank relied on a few large companies for their surplus food in addition to regular public administration support in the form of grants. In the last five years, the organisation has seen on the one hand an increase in efficiency and less wastage from the food sector, and, on the other, a weakening public sector. In response, the fundraising team has started to call upon a wider group of donors, including smaller companies who may donate more sporadically, and companies outside the food sector who may be able to help with specific needs such as new equipment, vehicles or maintenance costs. Most recently they have sought out individual donors, encouraging them to donate via simple online mechanisms. Between 2009 and 2010, the individual donations more than doubled, rising from €160,116.04 in 2009 to €422,608.39 in 2010.[34]

The financial opportunity presented by diverting waste from landfill is also being explored. In the UK, for example, the food bank Share Fare[35] is a profit-making business. An important part of its business model is based on the high landfill taxes that make it very expensive for supermarkets to dump their surplus. Fare Share offers the supermarket a service to deal with their waste for the same price as they would have to pay in Landfill Tax with the added benefit that the food is actually consumed rather than simply thrown away.

Finally, independence from public finance is also essential to the long-term economic sustainability of the Barcelona organisation, and over the years there has been a conscious shift away from public sector financial aid. While an annual grant is received, it is only a minor proportion of the Bank's income.

34 Barcelona Food Bank 2011 Annual Report

35 www.fareshare.org.uk

Innovation type

Campaigns similar to the Big Food Collection are run by the food banks across Europe; however, the Barcelona Food Bank's campaign stands out for its exponential growth over the last four years in mobilising volunteers, its communication capacity and its recent innovative introduction of online donations, as well as the more traditional practice of supermarket collections. This section explains how and why Barcelona is different.

Creativity and opportunity

Barcelona Food Bank has always striven to find creative, business-oriented solutions to help achieve its core objectives: the collection and fair redistribution of as much food as possible. One example of this creativity is the Bank's fruit juices and preserves initiative. Having observed the large quantity of fruit that went to waste in Spain, the Barcelona Food Bank discovered a small European Union grant for agricultural cooperatives, which is intended to save a percentage of producers' surplus fruit from being destroyed. Taking advantage of the Bank's network of food producers, a new initiative was set up to collect surplus fruit and convert it into juice and preserves. In the first year, 700,000 kg of fruit was collected for this purpose, which provided, on the one hand, an economically sustainable solution for farmers across Spain to deal with their surplus fruit and, on the other, income in the form of juice and preserves for the Food Bank to redistribute. The scheme has been running for three years now and, inspired by Barcelona, it has recently been adopted by the Food Bank in Italy.

Online donations

In 2010, the Barcelona Food Bank created an online donation system, via its own website, whereby individuals could choose from a series of specific products and brands to donate to the Food Bank from the comfort of their home or office. The donation is then registered by the relevant supermarket or company and remains in their stock until the Barcelona Food Bank decides to "cash it in". This provides the Bank with a virtual stock, which can be used to replenish the existing stock and particularly fill any nutritional gaps that might occur.

In 2011, the process of online donations was integrated into the Big Food Collection. Since the first campaign in 2009, the Big Food Collection has always had one main sponsor to cover the direct costs of the campaign (largely materials and logistics including boxes, crates, T-shirts, videos and transport). This sponsor has typically been a financial institution: first, Caixa Sabadell, then Unim; and, in the third year, the Foundation proposed La Caixa, one of Spain's largest financial institutions. In addition to sponsoring the direct costs of the campaign, Barcelona Food Bank proposed that La Caixa organise online donations through its various electronic channels, including a cashpoint donation service, online donations, mobile phone applications and other mechanisms. Food donated through La Caixa's electronic channels in the first year of its campaign amounted to 300,000 kg, around one-third of the total donations made during the campaign. The campaign is to be repeated in 2012.

La Caixa's online donation system is slightly different from that of the Barcelona Food Bank. However, the two run in parallel. The Caixa offers a series of "virtual baskets" of food at set prices, 10€, 20€, etc.

whereas the Foundation's system offers specific products from specific supermarkets, for example: 1 litre of Olive Oil from Condis, 6 tins of tuna from Caprabo, etc. The Barcelona Food Bank attracts those people who already know the Foundation and prefer to choose what they donate, while La Caixa reaches out to a far wider audience and although it is not such a transparent system, it is more successful at fundraising. However, what is of key importance in both cases is that the donations don't cost the Barcelona Food Bank anything in terms of campaign materials and so contribute to the organisation's overall economic efficiency.

> «The system meant that I could do what I know best (call people to collect kilos of food) and "La Caixa" calls people to donate online: it works perfectly! ... It's economically and environmentally perfect, I don't spend anything on cardboard or communication and above all it creates a current food account that we can draw upon whenever we need to, without worrying about the product reaching the end of its shelf-life.»
> —**Laia Guinjoan,** Director of Communications

Scalability and replicability

The Big Food Collection is a campaign that is replicated across European food banks. Barcelona learned from France and Portugal and, in turn, has helped Seville, in Southern Spain, to develop its own campaign. Based on Barcelona's experience, the following section outlines the key conditions for success and the management challenges other banks face in running similar campaigns.

Conditions for success

Barcelona Food Bank's experience has shown that it is necessary to have a series of core conditions to make the campaign work, which not every food bank may have in place.

> **Infrastructure:** the Bank needs to have a decent-sized warehouse space to classify the food as it comes in over a short period of time, and also needs to have considerable logistical support in terms of transport to collect the food from collection points and bring it to the classification point. Smaller food banks such as that in the city of Reus do not have this infrastructure.

> **Free distribution:** all of the food needs to be donated to the beneficiary; if a recipient organisation ends up selling the food, as has happened on occasions, the process gets muddled and the message is diluted. Ultimately, donors lose confidence and trust in the process. In the event that this happens the organisation in question should be removed from the system.

> **Rigour and efficiency:** a clear control system to ensure that the recipient organisations really do need the food and are not abusing the system, as in the case of the publicly funded old people's home, mentioned above.

Prestige and recognition: a close relationship with the local press, particularly individual journalists, and a very visible and clearly communicated campaign helps to achieve this.

Motivated team: an inspired, enthusiastic, hard-working and professional team working within a clear organisational structure towards a shared common purpose is essential for the campaign and the Food Bank's overall running. This includes rewarding volunteers.

Economic sustainability: a system based on goods being free – nothing bought, nothing sold – with diverse sources of income to cover minimum operational costs, independence from the public sector and business-oriented management.

Creativity: an eye for finding new sources of food and new sources of income, converting challenges into opportunities and being at the cutting edge of innovations in the sector.

Future impact

The target for 2013 is to reach 1,400 tons of food and 750 collection points with the long-term goal of involving every supermarket in Catalonia. Of the total of 3,000 supermarkets in Catalonia around 1,500 are suitable in that they are accessible for lorries, have sufficient storage space and can accommodate a collection box next to the till. The Barcelona Food Bank also aims to increase its stream of donations through online donations.

The Barcelona Food Bank has been inspired by the example of Portugal, where two Big Food Collections are organised each year with up to 25,000 volunteers, and it is currently involved in the organisation of a national Big Food Collection, which is led by the Federation of Food Banks in Spain. Forty-four of the 53 food banks across Spain have agreed to participate, and Barcelona continues to share its experience in this forum, although it is sceptical about how realistic a national campaign might be, given the above necessary conditions for success, and particularly the level of investment of people's time and the infrastructure that is needed for the campaign.

———

Appendix 1. Income and expenditure

The following tables show details of the Barcelona Food Bank's activities for 2010.

Table 13. Barcelona Food Bank income and expenditure

INCOME	2010 (€)	%	EXPENDITURE	2010 (€)	%
Department of Agriculture grants (to process fruit into juice)	203,764.49	18.8%	**Fruit processing** (into juice)	313,201.17	28.9%
European Union grants	392,563.00	36.2%	**Purchase of food**	124,972.27	11.5%
			Current activity	599,541.06	55.3%
Donations from businesses and banks	295,047.08	27.2%	**Repairs**	31,494.36	2.9%
			Total	1,083,409.15	
Individual and anonymous donations	127,561.31	11.8%			
Total	1,083,409.15				

Table 14. Barcelona Food Bank 2010 food income

FOOD DISTRIBUTED	KILOS	+/- SINCE 2009
Food collected	4,493,848	24%
EU programme	3,751,157	-3%
Total	8,245,005	10%

Table 15. Companies donating to the Barcelona Food Bank in 2010

ORIGIN OF FOOD COLLECTED	2010	%	ORIGIN OF FOOD COLLECTED	2010	%
Food industry (large scale)	2,769,432	61.63%	**Other food banks**	69,465	1.55%
			Operation Kilo	100,744	2.24%
Mercabarna (Barcelona markets)	542,804	12.08%	**Big Food Collection Aliments**	248,701	5.53%
Fruit recuperation programme	511,306	11.38%	**Schools**	47,386	1.05%
Fruit juice programme	129,800	2.59%	**"Tio Solidari" Catalonia Radio**	59,623	1.62%
Food industry (small scale)	10,414	0.23%	**Total**	4,493,848	

Table 16. Types of food donated to Barcelona Food Bank in 2010

MACRONUTRIENT	RDA%*	2010	KG TOTAL
Carbohydrates	60%	51.4%	4,237,933 kg
Fats	30%	37.6%	3,100,122 kg
Proteins	10%	10.9%	898,706 kg

* RDA is the daily recommended daily allowance expressed as a percentage for each macronutrient.

———

Appendix 2. Recipients, beneficiaries and volunteers

The following tables give details of the 308 organisations who received food donations in 2010. Some organisations belong to more than one type.

Table 17. Organisations receiving food from Barcelona Food Bank in 2010

FOOD DISTRIBUTION ACTIVITIES CARRIED OUT	NO. OF ORGANISATIONS	NO. OF BENEFICIARIES
Food parcels	236	90,937
Canteens	29	3,876
Breakfasts and afternoon snack	24	3,380
Sandwiches	2	206

Table 18. Types of beneficiary of Barcelona Food Bank in 2010

BENEFICIARY TYPE	NO.	BENEFICIARY TYPE	NO.
Individuals living below the poverty line	43,859	Ethnic minorities below the poverty line	1,579
Homeless people	4,267	Chronically ill	127
Women	374	Drug addicts	1,799
Children	2,236	People with AIDS	365
Young people	993	Immigrant-refugees and ethnic minorities	44,084
Elderly people	2,291	Individuals receiving support from religious organisations	368
Handicapped	1,101		
People living in temporary accommodation or waiting for housing support	193	Breastfeeding mothers	289
		Total	103,925

In Catalonia, the unemployment rate was 18% in 2010, with 1.5 million people, 20% of the population, living below the poverty line. In Spain as a whole this figure is 23%, with 10 million people living below the poverty line. Although the Barcelona Food Bank distributed food to 103,925 people in 2010, the numbers of families and single people in need have risen over the course of 2011 due to the rise in unemployment.

Table 19. Volunteers at the Barcelona Food Bank in 2010

AREA	NO. OF REGULAR VOLUNTEERS	AREA	NO. OF REGULAR VOLUNTEERS
Administration and finance	7	Fundraising	8
		Transport	7
European Union food	3	Human resource and volunteering	1
Suppliers	8		
Communication	4	Administrative support and telephone assistance	5
Local delegates	11		
Schools	6	Food security	3
Big Food Collection	8	Collaborators	4
Warehouse management	3	Distribution	10
Warehouse	28	Total	121
IT support	1		
Mercabarna (Barcelona markets)	4		

———

Appendix 3. Food wastage

The following tables show the origin of food wastage in Europe and Catalonia.

Table 20. Origin of wasted food in Europe

KG WASTED IN EUROPE*	89,000 MILLION	KG/PERSON
TOTAL POPULATION	501 MILLION	177.60
Food industry	39%	69.3
Restaurants & bars	14%	24.9
Business	5%	8.9
Domestic	42%	74.6
Totals	100%	177.6

Source: Agència de Residus, Catalonia
* Figures based on 550 kg consumed per person per year and include all types of food, organic, processed, etc.

Table 21. Origin of wasted food in Catalonia

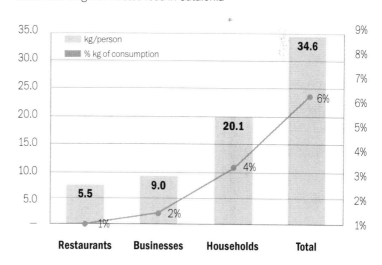

Source: Agència de Residus, Catalonia

———

References

Agència de Residus de Catalunya
www.arc-cat.net

Antoni Sansalvadó
President of Barcelona Food Bank, interviewed on 14th March 2012

Barcelona Food Bank (2012)
www.bancdelsaliments.org, accessed between December 2011 and March 2012

Barcelona Food Bank (2011)
2011 Annual Report

Barcelona Food Bank (2010)
2010 Annual Report

Barcelona Food Bank (2009)
2009 Annual Report

Big Food Collection Aliments (2012)
Press report from the 2011 Big Collection

Jordi Peix
Founder of Barcelona Food Bank, interviewed on 14th March 2012

Josué de Castro (1946)
The Geography of Hunger

Laia Guinjoan
Director of Communications for Barcelona Food Bank, interviewed on 14th March 2012

Behavioural Insights Team

«The Behavioural Insights Team was set up by the UK Government in July 2010 to find innovative and cost-effective ways to encourage support and enable people to make better choices for themselves. It is the first of its kind in the world.»
—**Cabinet Office,** 2010

Mission	Find innovative and cost-effective ways to encourage, support and enable people to make better choices for themselves
Founded	2010
Scalability	Replicable model for other national governments
Location	London, United Kingdom
Financing	Government funding of around £500,000 annually with the aim of achieving a ten fold return in two years
Social impact	National
Open Innovation	Yes
Innovation	Applying behavioural science to public policy

Introduction

The Behavioural Insights Team was set up by the UK Coalition Government in July 2010 to help meet its pledge to find *"intelligent ways to encourage, support and enable people to make better choices for themselves"*. The team's initial objectives were to transform at least two major areas of policy, spread awareness of behavioural economics[36] across government and achieve at least a tenfold return on the team's costs by July 2012, the point at which it would undergo its first review (Cabinet Office).

The Behavioural Insights Team is part of the UK government Cabinet Office. The Cabinet Office sits at the very centre of government, with an overarching purpose of making the government work better, supporting the Primer Minister and the Cabinet to ensure effective development, coordination and implementation of policy and operations across all government departments.[37] The Behavioural Insights Team is made up of eight people, civil servants and behavioural scientists. It is led by David Halpern, the former Chief Analyst of the Prime Minister's Strategy Unit and author of several publications on well-being and behavioural

---

36 *"Behavioural economics combines the twin disciplines of psychology and economics to explain why and how people make seemingly irrational or illogical decisions when they spend, invest, save, and borrow money"* (Belsky and Gilovich 1999).

37 www.cabinetoffice.gov.uk

change. He is closely connected to Richard Thaler[38] and other leading US-based behavioural scientists. The Team is supported by an Academic Advisory Group and overseen by a Steering Group chaired by the Cabinet Secretary, Jeremy Heywood. The Team's budget is approximately £500,000 per year.

In its first year of activity (2010–2011), the Team worked with a number of government departments to help them use behavioural insights to achieve a diverse range of objectives such as increasing the number of people on the organ donation registry, reducing alcohol consumption, providing consumers with access to the data businesses hold about them, collecting tax revenue on time, reducing fraud and cutting energy consumption.

Over the last 10 years, policy-makers have shown an increasing interest in, and enthusiasm for, the potential of behavioural economics to influence people's decisions and actions for individual welfare and the collective good,[39] particularly when designing public policy that depends on individuals' decision-making for its success. Behavioural theories have already been applied in the UK, the US and other countries to specific policy areas including crime prevention, recycling campaigns, responsible parenting, smoking cessation, reducing obesity and encouraging personal saving. These applications have been developed in order to redress the recognised limitations of hard policy instruments such as legislation and regulation to change people's behaviour. For example, the Department of Health, aware that age restrictions on purchasing tobacco and taxation is not enough to effectively reduce tobacco consumption, has for years run anti-smoking campaigns to gently encourage people to stop smoking through persuasive messages or information about smoking-related diseases (Behavioural Insights Team 2010).

> «We can all cite instances in which we know that we should act differently in our own self-interest or in the wider interest, but for one reason or another do not. The traditional tools of government have proven to be less successful in addressing these behavioural problems. We need to think about ways of supplementing the more traditional tools of government, with policy that helps to encourage behaviour change of this kind.»
> —**Gus O'Donnell,** former Cabinet Secretary and Head of Civil Service

The New Economics Foundation has distilled concepts from behavioural economics down to seven key principles, which are useful to consider when designing public policy.

---

38 Richard Thaler is Professor of Behavioural Science and Economics at the University of Chicago Booth School of Business and author of *Nudge* as well as numerous publications on behavioural finance.

39 Behavioural economics takes into consideration behavioural science and social psychology to better understand the motivations for economic decision-making. Applying this field to public policy has been described as "libertarian paternalism" whereby individuals are gently pushed or "nudged" into making choices that will ultimately benefit themselves as individuals and may have positive knock-on impacts for society (Thaler & Sunstein 2008).

Box 1. The seven principles of behavioural economics

1 **Other people's behaviour matters:** people do many things by observing others and copying; people are encouraged to continue doing things when they feel other people approve of their behaviour.

2 **Habits are important:** people do many things without consciously thinking about them. These habits are hard to change – even though people might want to change their behaviour, it is not easy for them.

3 **People are motivated to "do the right thing":** there are cases where money is de-motivating as it undermines people's intrinsic motivation; for example, you would quickly stop inviting friends to dinner if they insisted on paying you.

4 **People's self-expectations influence how they behave:**
they want their actions to be in line with their values and their commitments.

5 **People are loss-averse and hang on to what they consider "theirs".**

6 **People are bad at computation when making decisions:** they put undue weight on recent events and too little on far-off ones; they cannot calculate probabilities well and worry too much about unlikely events; and they are strongly influenced by how the problem/information is presented to them.

7 **People need to feel involved and effective to make a change:**
just giving people the incentives and information is not necessarily enough.

Source: New Economics Foundation 2005

Achievements and progress made

The Behavioural Insights Team has made significant progress in the areas of public health, the environment, consumer empowerment, and fraud and error. These are the priority areas that were set out by the Team's steering group.[40] Various policy interventions have been trialled in these areas and show potential for major cost savings and considerable behavioural change to achieve the targeted policy objectives. In addition work has begun on crime, charitable giving, social mobility, relationships and parenting, wellbeing and public service reform.

Before setting up the Team, a review of behavioural economics was commissioned to analyse progress made both in the UK and abroad. Based on this research a set of practical guidelines, the MINDSPACE framework, was produced, which sets out how behavioural theories can be applied to all areas of public policy. This report concluded that although behavioural approaches provide a potentially powerful set of new tools, in order to encourage a greater uptake of the behavioural economic theories across government policy-makers first need to recognise that they are in the business of influencing behaviour (Institute for Government 2009). The Team has used the MINDSPACE framework to help encourage the uptake of behavioural economics across government.

---

40 See Table 23 for highlights of these achievements.

Table 22. MINDSPACE framework

Messenger	We are heavily influenced by those who communicate information
	Using mothers in gang-related crime prevention has been shown to cause up to 70% reduction in youth homicides (Ceasefire, US).
Incentives	Our responses to incentives are shaped by predictable mental shortcuts such as strongly avoiding losses
	Reverse vending machines that return money to the consumer for empty containers has shown up to a 70% return rate (AG Barr 2007).
Norms	We are strongly influenced by what others do
	Partners of individuals who face a workplace smoking ban are 40% more likely to quit (Duncan, Haller & Porters 1968).
Defaults	We "go with the flow" of pre-set options
	Countries with "opt out" organ donation systems have much higher (around 70%) uptake than those with "opt in" systems (around 30%) (Organ Donation Taskforce 2008).
Salience	Our attention is drawn to what is novel and seems relevant to us
	Putting the tax on a product label rather than adding it at the register has been effective for reducing alcohol consumption in the US (Chetty, Looney & Croft 2009).
Priming	Our acts are often influenced by subconscious cues
	Reduce the size of food containers to reduce obesity (moviegoers eat 45% more popcorn when given in a larger container, even if stale!) (Wansink and Kim 2006).
Affect	Our emotional associations can powerfully shape our actions
	Bringing offenders face to face with their victims to evoke anger or guilt has proved effective in restorative justice schemes (Home Affairs Select Committee 2009).
Commitments	We seek to be consistent with our public promises, and reciprocate acts
	Smoking quitters who deposit monthly payments in a savings account (to be returned if they successfully quit) has helped people give up smoking (Gine, Karlan & Zinman 2008).
Ego	We act in ways that make us feel better about ourselves
	The campaign to reduce speeding by male drivers, which used a woman gesturing with her finger to signal that driving fast is to compensate for having a small penis, has proven effective (Bullock & Jones 2004).

MINDSPACE: *A checklist of influences on our behaviour for use when making policy, developed on the basis of research from social psychology, cognitive psychology and behavioural economics.*

Table 23. Highlights of achievements of the Behavioural Insights Team 2010–2011

INTERVENTIONS	BEHAVIOURAL THEORY APPLIED	POTENTIAL IMPACT
Organ donation		
Include **required choice** for organ donation for online vehicle licence applications; applicants have to choose whether or not to donate their organs in the case of an accident, rather than having to "opt in" of their own accord.	Unless prompted to choose people tend to go with the **default** option – which in England was to opt out of the organ registry unless proactively opting in. Trials show people are much more likely to opt in to the register if they are required to make a choice.	This scheme was implemented in 2010 and is expected to double the proportion joining the organ register to 70% of all applicants, equating to 1 million extra donors over a two-year period.
Alcohol consumption		
Reduce alcohol "dosage" through **smaller portion** sizes using smaller glasses in pubs · **Lower default alcohol strengths** in certain brands of beer · Advertising campaign in universities to **correct false perceptions** of drinking levels.	Our tendency to **default** shows we remain faithful to a brand even if its characteristics change. Social **norms** mean we copy what we see, but perceptions are often distorted through the **salient** behaviour of a few, so we think people drink more than they do and copy this behaviour.	Heineken's "Responsibility Deal" pledge to remove 100m units of alcohol amounts to reducing total UK alcohol intake by 0.3%. University campaigns in other countries have shown considerable reduction in consumption.
Energy efficiency		
Redesign Energy Performance Certificates for homes with **clearer information** and greater focus on costs and potential savings · Install smart meters **comparing consumption** to the average and give **positive feedback** when reducing consumption.	We tend to strongly avoid loss so attention to the costs of heating a home is an **incentive** for action. If information is made relevant and set out clearly it becomes more **salient** to us. According to social **norms** we are influenced by what others do and therefore we act in ways that make us feel better.	1.4m households will receive the new certificate and two major utilities companies will use smart meters in 2012. This could influence people's buying and renting decisions and property prices. In the Netherlands homes with a green label sell at a premium of 3.6%.

INTERVENTIONS	BEHAVIOURAL THEORY APPLIED	POTENTIAL IMPACT
Consumer empowerment		
Design of "Mydata" online system enabling consumers to access, control and use data held about them by businesses, enabling more informed choices on mobile phone contracts, fat content of food, credit card contracts or pensions.	**Inertia** makes it difficult for consumers to switch suppliers, which can make it difficult for new, innovative businesses to establish themselves. Information that is **salient**, well presented and easily comparable generates more trust so consumers are empowered to switch to a better deal.	76% of mobile phone users are on the wrong contract and 26% of consumers get a worse deal when switching energy suppliers. Empowering consumers to choose a better deal is expected to stimulate business growth and innovation better suited to people's needs across sectors.
Reduce fraud		
Change letters to people who have not paid their self-assessment tax, simplifying messages and explaining that others in their area have already paid.	People are strongly influenced by what others do and the use of a **positive social norm** has been shown to be very effective in changing people's behaviour in various situations. Research also shows that we are more likely to be honest if we sign up-front.	140,000 debts worth £290m were trialled with an increase of £350m tax paid in the first six weeks of the campaign. Repayment rates are expected to increase by 15% and £30m of extra revenue expected per year if rolled out to all self-assessment customers.

Source: Behavioural Insights Team 2010

Impact and degree of transformation

The greatest impact of the Behavioural Insights Team can be analysed from three perspectives: first, the *cultural shift* that has taken place in certain government departments that are engaging with the use of behavioural theories in their policy-making practice in a more proactive and methodological way than before; second, the potential identified for *cost savings* particularly in the area of tax, error and fraud; and, third, the potential for change in *lifestyle choices* contributing to both individual and social well-being.

Cultural shift among policy makers
«When the team was set up, some government departments were relatively sceptical. We are now inundated with requests from officials looking at ways of applying insights from behavioural science or seeking to understand how to test and trial new interventions.»
—**Owain Service,** Deputy Director Behavioural Insights Team

The Behavioural Insights Team has been very successful at raising the profile of behavioural and experimental work across government, and this has resulted in some government departments setting up their own internal teams to apply behavioural insight to the policy design process. For example, HM Revenue and Customs (HMRC) has set up a Behaviour Change Unit, there is a new team within the Department of Energy and Climate Change which focuses on customer insight and a behavioural economics "Incubator Unit" has been set up within the Department of Business, Innovation and Skills.

Although behavioural theories had previously been applied sporadically across the UK government – for example, in certain local authorities, the Department of International Development and the Pensions Commission – prior to the creation of the team the concepts had not been systematically or strategically applied by central government. In addition, the work carried out had not always been robustly measured or given high-level political support.

One example of the more strategic uptake of behavioural economics is the application of the MINDSPACE framework by the Department for Business, Innovation and Skills consumer empowerment strategy ("Better Choices, Better Deals"), which is part of the overarching economic policy "Plan for Growth" (Behavioural Insights Team and Department for Business 2011). This strategy is an example of how a government department is making a conscious shift away from previous hard policy instruments such as regulation and taxation, towards a new approach, which aims to facilitate and encourage businesses, regulators and consumer groups to work together to address common challenges based on a better understanding of the psychology of decision-making.

The aim of the Consumer Empowerment Strategy is twofold: on the one hand to provide consumers with better information and opportunities to make better purchasing deals and, on the other, to stimulate business growth and innovation with little cost and no regulation.[41] Behavioural concepts from MINDSPACE have been woven into the strategy, above all the recognition that consumers do not always respond in an economically rational way to financial or other incentives. For example, as we often do not have the time, desire or cognitive resources to make a fully informed decision if we collaborate with others in our purchasing, the cost of making such decisions can be reduced (Behavioural Insights Team 2011).

---

41 The theory underpinning the strategy is that more empowered consumers will drive business efficiency, thereby fostering a greater market share for those businesses that offer the best services and products, which will squeeze out lower-quality products and reduce incumbent advantages (Behavioural Insights Team 2010).

Table 24. Highlights of behavioural economics from the Consumer Empowerment Strategy

POLICY AREA	BETTER INFORMATION	COLLABORATIVE CONSUMPTION
Intervention	Lowest energy tariff information: Give consumers clearer information about the lowest available tariff on energy bills and assistance with switching provider. Trial under way to be reviewed after two years.	Collective purchasing innovation prize: Produce an advice toolkit with information to support new collective purchasing initiatives and a prize of £30,000 for those who build communities to stimulate collective purchasing.
Partners	*Energy Retailers Association, six largest energy suppliers in the UK*	*Community networks, business associations, consumer organisations, cooperative associations*
Intervention	Annual credit card statements: Produce 12-month statements on credit card payments with clearer information about fees and how to switch to better deals, information to customers who make low payments and changes in interest rates.	Collective green purchasing: Offer incentives to neighbourhoods to buy collectively environmental products such as loft insulation and energy-efficient products, making the products cheaper as more people buy them.
Partners	*UK Cards Association*	*Homebase, Argos, B&Q*
Behavioural concepts applied	Information presented in clear, relevant, trustworthy ways is more **salient** to us. Research shows consumers often get a worse deal when switching provider as information is unclear. As we are averse to loss, by showing 12-month costs of credit cards is a greater **incentive** to switch supplier; however, our inertia, and tendency to **default** means it is difficult to switch providers and we need help with this.	Consumers often feel they do not have the time or energy required to make logical, informed purchasing decisions, but when consumers collaborate the cost of these efforts can be spread out resulting in better prices and higher efficiency. Discounts for otherwise risk-averse investments, such as loft insulation, are an **incentive** for consumers as up-front rewards are more salient than long-term savings and we follow the trend set by social **norms** and by our peers.

Source: Behavioural Insights Team 2010

Cost savings

In its first two years, the Behavioural Insights Team has identified savings that amount to well over £20m in direct cash savings, but, given that the interventions will deliver longer-term benefits, the overall cost savings of interventions now in place will amount to many hundreds of millions of pounds. The most significant direct savings identified are in the area of Customs and Revenue, particularly related to tax and fraud. Simple, cost-effective measures have been trialled in these areas, such as subtly changing the language used in letters and thereby encouraging people to pay their tax.

In February 2011, the Behavioural Insights Team supported HMRC in a trial to establish the impact of altering the messages sent in letters to encourage tax debtors to pay the tax they owed and, by April of the same year, a trial of 140,000 self-assessment tax debts worth £290 million was carried out. The results showed that letters which informed people that the majority of people in their area had already paid their tax and reminded them of the benefits of paying tax for their local area out performed those who received the standard letters as shown in Figure 13. Variations of the letters were sent out to test people's reaction to the behaviour of other taxpayers nationally, in their postcode or in their town. The trial showed that people were more likely to change their behaviour when the letter mentioned people in their town. HMRC estimates that this effect, if rolled out and repeated across the country, could advance approximately £160 million of tax debts to the Exchequer over the six-week period of the trial. This would free up collector resource capable of generating £30 million of extra revenue annually.

HMRC also carried out a wider self-assessment debt campaign and increased income by more than £350 million in the first six weeks of the campaign, trebling the amount collected over the same period the previous year. Building on the success of these trials and harnessing the potential of social norms to encourage payment, the HMRC is investigating other areas of potential savings in the area of debt and fraud. Early results show that people prefer the use of encouraging letters to the previous more heavy-handed penalty approach (Behavioural Insights Team 2011).

Figure 13. Using social norms to encourage tax debt payment

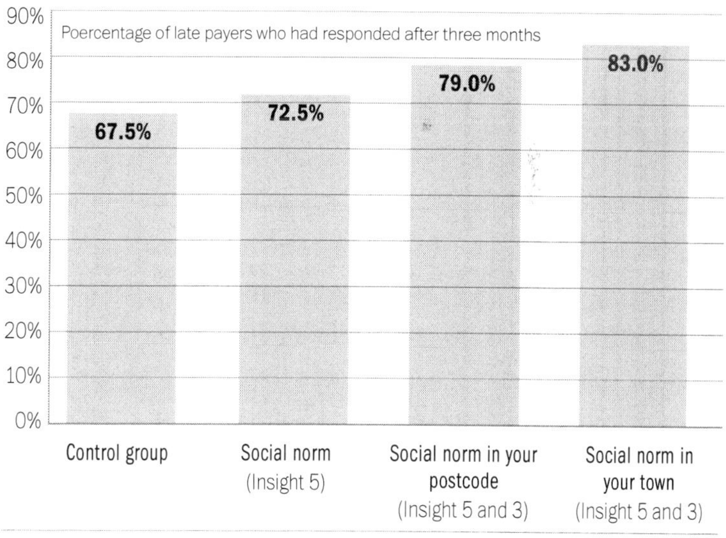

Poercentage of late payers who had responded after three months

Control group: 67.5%
Social norm (Insight 5): 72.5%
Social norm in your postcode (Insight 5 and 3): 79.0%
Social norm in your town (Insight 5 and 3): 83.0%

Source: Behavioural Insights Team 2012 (a)

The potential of these savings has been identified through the application of randomised control trials. While previous work in this field may have used elements of behavioural economics, it was rarely tested or trialled in a significantly robust way or on a statistically relevant scale.

Box 2. Randomised control trials

Randomised controlled trials (RCTs) are the best way of determining whether a policy is working. They are now used extensively in international development, medicine and business to identify which policy, drug or sales method is most effective. In its most recent publication – "Test, Learn, Adapt" – the Behavioural Insights Team makes the case for RCTs being used much more widely in all areas of public policy.

What makes RCTs different from other types of evaluation is the introduction of a randomly assigned control group, which enables you to compare the effectiveness of a new intervention against what would have happened if you had changed nothing. The introduction of a control group eliminates a whole host of biases that normally complicate the evaluation process – for example, if you introduce a new "back to work" scheme, how will you know whether those receiving the extra support might not have found a job anyway?

With the right academic and policy support, the Team believes that RCTs can be much cheaper and simpler to put in place than is often supposed. By demonstrating how well a policy is working, RCTs can save money in the long term. They are a powerful tool to help policy-makers and practitioners decide which of several policies is the most cost-effective, and also which interventions are not as effective as might have been supposed.

The Team has identified nine separate steps that are required to set up any RCT. Many of these steps will be familiar to anyone putting in place a well-designed policy evaluation – for example, the need to be clear, from the outset, about what the policy is seeking to achieve. Some of them, in particular the need to randomly allocate individuals or institutions to different groups which receive different treatment, are what lend RCTs their power. The nine steps are at the heart of the Behavioural Insights Team's test, learn, adapt methodology, which focuses on understanding better what works and continually improving policy interventions to reflect what we have learnt. They are described below.

Test

1. Identify two or more policy interventions to compare (e.g. old vs new policy; different variations of a policy).
2. Determine the outcome that the policy is intended to influence and how it will be measured in the trial.
3. Decide on the randomisation unit: whether to randomise to intervention and control groups at the level of individuals, institutions (e.g. schools), or geographical areas (e.g. local authorities).
4. Determine how many units (people, institutions or areas) are required for robust results.
5. Assign each unit to one of the policy interventions, using a robust randomisation method.
6. Introduce the policy interventions to the assigned groups.

Learn

7. Measure the results and determine the impact of the policy interventions.

Adapt

8. Adapt your policy intervention to reflect your findings.
9. Return to Step 1 to continually improve your understanding of what works.

Test, Learn, Adapt: Developing Public Policy with Randomised Control Trials (Cabinet Office 2012 (b))

Each year in the UK, £21 billion is lost to fraud in the public sector, a further £9.6 billion is lost as a result of errors, while £7–8 billion is lost in uncollected debt.[42] The Team has identified potential cost savings by exploring ways to reduce fraud, error and debt, and in their recent report on this subject the Team highlights seven insights that can be used to achieve these cost savings. Some of these insights have already been tested with remarkable results as shown in Figure 14 where doctors who receive simplified letters to remind them to pay their tax show a far higher response rate than those who received the standard correspondence.

Box 3. Seven Insights to reduce fraud, error and debt

Insight 1. Make it easy: Make it as straightforward as possible for people to pay tax or debts: for example, by pre-populating a form with information already held.

Insight 2. Highlight key messages: Draw people's attention to important information or actions required of them: for example, by highlighting them up-front in a letter.

Insight 3. Use personal language: Personalise language so that people understand why a message or process is relevant to them.

Insight 4. Prompt honesty at key moments: Ensure that people are prompted to be honest at key moments when filling in a form or answering questions.

Insight 5. Tell people what others are doing: Highlight the positive behaviour of others: for instance, that "9 out of 10 people pay their tax on time".

Insight 6. Reward desired behaviour: Actively incentivise or reward behaviour that saves time or money.

Insight 7. Highlight the risk and impact of dishonesty: Emphasise the impact of fraud or late payment on public services, as well as the risk of audits and the consequences for those caught.

It is important to remember that the effectiveness of the application of these insights will heavily depend on the context in which they are applied.

Behavioural Insights Team 2012 (a)

---

42 Cabinet Office Taskforce on Fraud, Error and Debt (2012), *Reducing Fraud & Error in Government;* Cabinet Office Taskforce on Fraud, Error and Debt (2012), *Tackling Debt Owed to Central Government.*

Figure 14. Response rate of doctors to HMRC letters

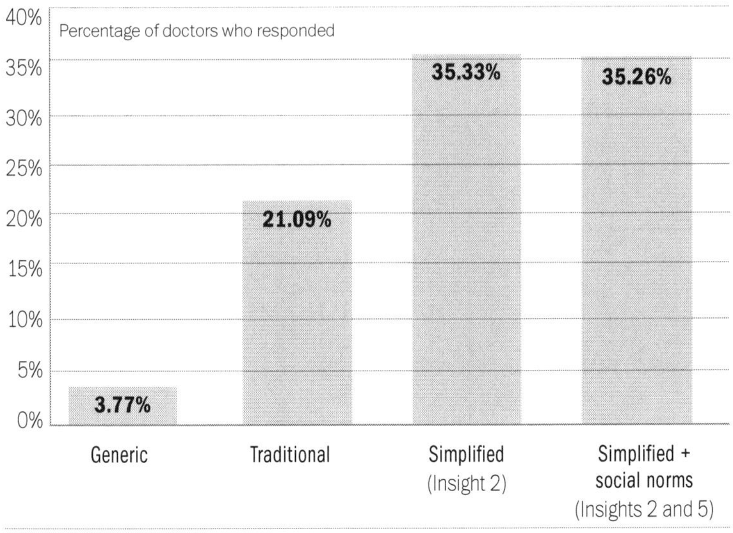

Source: Behavioural Insights Team 2012 (a)

Change in lifestyle choices

The Team's work in the area of public health has shown that some of the most significant ways of influencing people's lifestyle choices are through applying cost-effective non-regulatory measures. These are based on behavioural economics, as well as existing research and expertise provided by the Department of Health and other partners. Lifestyle factors that impact upon people's health, such as not having a balanced diet, doing too little exercise or drinking too much, are very hard to tackle with regulation, hence the need for a far more profound understanding of social psychology and behavioural science. These issues are estimated to cost the National Health Service (NHS) a considerable amount of money.

«Six out of ten adults are overweight, costing the UK economy around £7 billion per year. (...) Alcohol-related illness costs the NHS around £2.7 billion a year. (...) There are over a million cases of food poisoning a year in the UK, costing the NHS and business £1.5 billion.»
—**Cabinet Office,** 2010

Figure 15. Bayer's Nintendo Didget device for diabetic children

Bayer Healthcare and Nintendo DS have developed a device to make regular blood-sugar testing fun for children. The Didget device gives points which can be used on Nintendo games in return for regular pin-prick blood-sugar tests.

The public health policy interventions in which the Team has been involved are guided by the philosophy set out by the Team's Director , David Halpern, who is author of numerous publications on well-being and behaviour change. Halpern argues that policy outcomes will be much enhanced by citizens' participation; that there are strong moral and political arguments for protecting and enhancing personal responsibility; and that behaviour-based interventions can be significantly more cost-effective than traditional service delivery. Examples of the Team's involvement in this area include the following:

Smoking: The Team is working in partnership with Boots (the leading chain of High Street pharmacists in the UK) and the Department of Health to develop a new smoking cessation trial, combining behavioural interventions with pharmacological support and building on the existing NHS-commissioned stop-smoking services that are already provided in the Boots stores.

Alcohol: The Team is implementing a two-year campaign trial with Welsh universities to correct the false perception that other students drink more than they actually do, in order to reduce alcohol consumption in young people. In addition, agreements have been made with key brands such as Heineken, to reduce the strength of certain beers and with the supermarkets Waitrose, Asda and Morrisons to remove alcohol from the front of their stores.

Diet and weight: In collaboration with Asda, we tested the UK Department of Health's "Change for Life" campaign, which consists of social messages on shopping carts that encourage consumers to buy healthier products. BIT is also seeking to collaborate with other partners to launch similar initiatives, such as creating specific shopping-cart compartments for fruits and vegetables and changing the location of healthy products on supermarket shelves.

Physical activity: In partnership with Nike, an application for the iPhone has been developed to encourage children to walk to school more often; the children get points for every lamp-post they pass on the way to school and to compete against classmates with prizes (e.g. cinema tickets). The Team is exploring how similar initiatives could be scaled up and implemented in collaboration with local authorities and other actors.

Food hygiene: In an attempt to reduce the cost of food poisoning, the Team is working with the Food Standards Agency to make the information generated by the new National Food Hygiene Rating System as widespread and accessible as possible, brokering partnerships with restaurant reviewers such as Time Out, the Good Food Guide and Top Table to rank restaurants on their hygiene standards as well as the quality of food and service.

Figure 16. Step2Get and Nike App to encourage pupils to walk to school

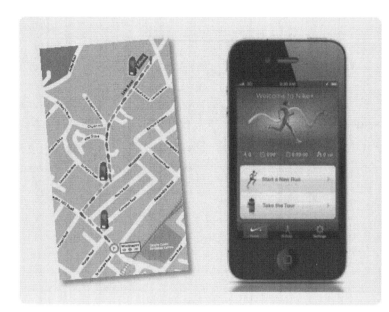

Step2Get combines online gaming, mobile technology and swipe cards to encourage pupils to walk to school. Pupils swipe lamp-posts on their way to school to gain points in a competition where they can win cinema or Topshop vouchers. A similar scheme is linked to Nike's running app for youth running competitions.

The work done by the team in raising awareness of the need to study the psychological aspects and motivations behind changes in lifestyle has resulted in the creation of a new Policy Research Unit on Behaviour and Health. This systematises the work across the sector and uses robust experimentation techniques.

Cross-sector collaboration

The Behavioural Insights Team was conceived as a small, agile unit to act as a catalyst for spreading behavioural practice across government departments and to forge partnerships with other sectors. To achieve this vision, the Team has followed an engagement process comprising the following steps: raising awareness, brokering partnerships, demonstrating potential through trials, communicating the results to engage organisations from within government and among businesses and civil society organisations and, finally, embedding the approach in the policy-making process.

Step 1: Raising awareness

The Team carried out a series of seminars across Whitehall to highlight the significance and potential for behavioural economics in public policy. The involvement of recognised experts such as Richard Thaler and other UK academics working in this field was useful at this stage as was the use of innovative examples of how behavioural science has been used in other countries. For example, in 2011, the Team was featured in a Radio 4 documentary exploring the interface between behavioural science and public policy. In collaboration with the National School for Government, the Team disseminated its policy and methodology papers, such as "Test, Learn, Adapt", to policy-makers and the public. In addition to this, the team produces a bulletin to keep policy-makers informed of the latest research in behavioural science, and holds weekly brainstorm sessions to help civil servants and other public sector workers think through their policy challenges using the tools of behavioural science.

Step 2: Brokering partnerships

Agreements or partnerships with other parts of government, typically a department, were established to identify the key policy areas to be targeted and the relevant actors to engage with. For example, within the Department of Energy and Climate Change the two major policy areas, Green Deal and Smart Meters, were identified as opportunities for intervention and the teams approached were the Strategy and Policy Team and Customer Insight Team respectively. Once interest had been sparked and a policy area identified, the Team would often broker a partnership between the Department and other relevant stakeholders to design an appropriate collective intervention. This involved businesses, regulatory bodies and civil society organisations and, in some cases, international agents.

One example of the Team brokering a partnership with businesses or government departments was in the area of health. Potential benefits to business of engaging in this type of partnership are credibility, corporate social responsibility, reputation and the potential to scale the product or service in question. An example is offered by the case of Nintendo, which developed the Didget device to encourage children with diabetes to test their blood-sugar level more regularly and thereby addressed a recognised problem of the many children that end up in hospital due to infrequent testing.

One of the most ambitious of the Behavioural Insights Team's partnerships with the private sector has been with the Department for Business, Innovation and Skills' Mydata initiative, which works with over 20 leading businesses, covering financial services, retail, utilities, telecoms and online platforms, and consumer groups. The Information Commissioner's Office, which is the UK's independent authority for upholding information rights, is involved in helping consumers' access, control and use data held about them by businesses (Behavioural Insights Team 2010). Another outcome of the partnerships with businesses is a series of voluntary agreements: Heineken's pledge to reduce the alcohol strength of one of its major brands; ASDA's pledge not to display alcohol in the foyer of its stores; and 80 organisations have signed up to a pledge to make staff restaurants healthier. To encourage all these businesses' commitments pledge delivery plans are to be published by the Department of Health as part of the Responsibility Deal (Cabinet Office 2010).

Step 3: Demonstrating potential

The third step marks the most innovative aspect of the Team's work, whereby the potential for achieving policy objectives is demonstrated through the design, implementation and analysis of a trial of the different interventions proposed. The aforementioned work with HMRC in encouraging people to pay their tax on time is an example of how the potential of the intervention has already been demonstrated by the figures for revenue generated. In the case of organ donations, the trial being carried out is with online driving licence applications. If it proves successful it will also be scaled up to paper licence applications. Some trials, such as the Credit Card Annual Statement, have been held over periods of up to two years, and others used large groups of up to 100,000 participants. Many trials used RCTs and some included AB testing, whereby different messages are used in parallel to constantly test and improve the messages of particular campaigns. In the environmental sector, the latest energy paper contains a set of trials conducted in partnership with businesses (such as B&Q, Homebase and Opower) and with local councils (such as Sutton, Kingston and Merton).

Step 4: Communicating the results

The Team has published six policy papers, often in collaboration with the relevant department, to communicate the results achieved to date and to advocate new ways of working. These papers help to formalise the partnerships established between the Team and the different government departments. They also serve as strategic planning tools, helping to prioritise and organise the work to be carried out and raise awareness of the potential of behavioural economics both in the department in question and other areas of government that are being encouraged to undergo a similar process. Four papers have been published to date. The Team receives many requests to begin work in new fields and it has been asked to produce guidance for local authorities on how to use evidence effectively and how to ensure that data collection and reporting is of a sufficiently high quality to enable comparisons and analysis and for the results to be transferable to other local authorities.

Box 4. Policy papers published 2010–2011

Applying Behavioural Insight to Health

published in December 2010.

Behaviour Change and Energy Use

was published with Department of Energy and Climate and Communities and Local Government in July 2011.

Better Choices: Better Deals. Consumers Powering Growth

was published with Department for Business, Innovation and Skills in April 2011.

Applying behavioural Insights to Reduce Fraud, Error and Debt

was published in April 2012.

Test, Learn, Adapt: Developing Public Policy with Randomised Control Trials

was published in early 2012 and has already been downloaded 20,000 times.

Step 5. Embedding the approach

The final step was for the relevant government department or business to take ownership of the behavioural approach and adopt their own long-term mechanism to address policy in this way. This was achieved by the Department of Energy and Climate Change, which established a Customer Insight Team, and by HMRC, which set up a Behaviour Change Unit. Once the departments have been empowered in this way to integrate behavioural economics into their own policy design process, the Team can move on to other areas, as is already happening. To help facilitate this final step, the Behavioural Science in Government Network has been formed. It is led by the Government's Economic and Social Research Services and has representatives from many departments. Through this network, the Team can promote effective evaluation of behavioural interventions, share reports, events and information.

Economic sustainability and long-term viability

The Behavioural Insights Team was set up in a climate of austerity and public spending cuts and one of its core objectives has been that the government savings it identifies should have a value of ten times its own budget over the two-year period. Significantly it has been given from the outset a defined timescale of two years, after which it will be evaluated by the Government Steering Group to assess impact and effectiveness and to decide upon its future strategy. The annual budget is approximately £500,000, which covers fixed overheads (desks, telephones, IT) and all other costs.

The so-called "Sunset Review" is a mechanism that has been put in place to avoid the tendency to default, which in this case would mean to continue to run the Team under the same conditions, regardless of its achievements. Experience shows that when a new department is created it is often easier to allow it to continue to exist rather than going through the effort of shutting it down. According to Peter John, a member of the Academic Advisory Group, there is a possibility the Team will be invited to continue for another year, however, the review has been put in place so that the default option is that the Team ceases to exist rather than the opposite.

Cost savings on public expenditure

Cost savings to the public purse have been identified by the Team on a variety of levels and below are examples of the different strategies adopted.

Fraud, debt and error

Where most savings have been identified is in the area of fraud, debt and error. As is shown in Figure 11, significant potential savings have been made through the use of social norms to encourage people to pay their tax payments on time, simple and collective messages used to encourage tax payment and personal text messages to encourage the payment of fines.

Public health

Public health is another area that represents a major opportunity for cost savings, although in this case it is more difficult to measure. In the policy report "Applying Behavioural Insight to Public Health" the Team provides a series of figures regarding public health expenditure for lifestyle-related issues such as illnesses related to alcohol, smoking and obesity. The report also states that the government could save an additional £900 million per year if people who engage in low levels of physical activity were more active (Wanless 2004).

Given that many public health issues involve the consumption of products, such as salt, alcohol and cigarettes, the involvement of the private sector is crucial in this sphere and the Team's success in partnering with businesses to address health-related challenges will be crucial to their success. If the Team is able to identify similar estimates for savings in the field of public health, as it has done in the areas of tax and fraud, the potential for its progress in this area is huge.

The engagement of the Department of Health in behavioural economics is another key indicator of the long-term viability of the Team's work. The Department of Health has also set up the Behaviour Change Network, chaired by the Director General for Public Health and has also invested £5m over five years in the Policy Research Unit on Behaviour and Health to help generate evidence on the effectiveness, value for money and impact on health inequalities interventions (Cabinet Office 2010).

Table 25. Trials carried out to reduce fraud, error and debt

BEHAVIOURAL APPROACH	OBJECTIVE	TARGET SAMPLE	RESULTS	POTENTIAL SAVING
1. Using social norms	Does informing people that the majority of neighbours have already paid their tax significantly boost payment rates?	140,000 taxpayers	15% increase in paying on time with social norms including "9 out of 10 have already paid" in a letter.	Potential for £30m extra annual revenue if scaled up.
2. Highlighting key messages and norms	Can tax compliance be increased among doctors by simplifying the principal messages and actions required?	3,000 doctors	29% increase in paying tax with 1,500 doctors coming forward.	£1m in voluntary tax declarations already made.
3. Using salient images	Do images help to reduce repeat correspondence and encourage prompt payment of driving related fines?	Not specified	Trial ongoing with different messages, showing use of photos of the car and driver to be most effective.	
4. Better presentation of information	What is the most effective way of presenting information to encourage problematic tax payments?	39,000 taxpayers	25% more paid their debt with collective messages.	Could annually accelerate £80 million in cashflow by at least ten days, freeing up collector resources to pursue other debts.
5. Personalising text messages	What is the impact of sending personalised text messages on people's likelihood of paying court ordered fines?	1,000 SMS per month in 3 different regions	Early results show a 28% increase in payment when the person's name is used in text messages compared to no message at all.	
6. Prompting honesty	Does simplifying messages, emphasising consequences and signing up-front result in more honesty?	38,000 letters	Early results show a 6% drop in requests to repeat tax deduction for a single person with salient information and potential risk of non-compliance included in letter.	
7. Varying the tone of letters	Which type of communication is more effective to get plumbers to get their tax affairs up to date?	12,000 plumbers	Trial ongoing using three different letter types with traditional, direct and cooperative language.	
8. Using beliefs about tax	What are the more effective messages to get companies to pay their tax debts?	32,000 companies	Early results show more debt payment when the gap between individual's belief and company practice is highlighted.	

Source: Behavioural Insights Team 2012 (a). The figures here have be calculated on the basis of those given in the report "Applying Behavioural Insights to Reduce Fraud, Error and Debt."

Environment

There is a wealth of research on the potential for behavioural shifts to reduce the economic cost of environmental issues caused by individual choices, from the macro level, such as the Stern Review's analysis of the cost of climate change to the UK economy, to the micro level, such as an individual council's street cleaning costs estimated at £547m in 2005–2006.[43] The Team is building on research from the Departments of Energy and Climate and Food, Farming and Rural Affairs on how best to influence behaviour to achieve environmental objectives and cost savings, in a variety of areas including energy and water use, mobility, recycling, and consumption. It is channelling this work through the new policy to be launched in 2012, the Green Deal. The value added by the Team is to ensure that future interventions proposed are as effective as possible and based on robust research.

Another example of environment-related cost saving is the government's own energy bill where a reduction of 14% in energy consumption has already been achieved in comparison to consumption between 2010 and 2011. The most successful measures included changing the default energy settings in government buildings to mesh them more tightly with actual consumption, as well as showing comparative consumption data across departments as a way of generating a sense of competition. Savings achieved so far amount to £13 million per year.

Saving money for individuals

As well as identifying areas where the government can save money, the Team has also been active in finding opportunities to help individuals save money, particularly through the Consumer Empowerment Strategy and in the realm of energy efficiency and climate change. The potential value of savings for individuals from Mydata, which was launched in 2012, is very wide-ranging. It includes the possibility of identifying which of 2 million mobile phone contracts is most suitable for them based on their last 12 months' usage, or facilitating the switch to a better credit card contract or lower energy tariff.

Green collective purchasing schemes are another area of potential savings for the consumer. These have been designed in collaboration with businesses such as B&Q and Homebase. The schemes give consumers discounts if they are recommended by their neighbours or are part of a collective purchasing scheme. Such campaigns have included sending letters to neighbourhoods to encourage the uptake of particular energy-efficiency products and the more the neighbours take part in the scheme, the more the price of the product is reduced.

The long-term viability of the Team will ultimately be demonstrated when it is no longer needed. The viability of the Team's work ultimately depends on their capacity to integrate a behavioural approach into government departments and to convince departments to design their interventions on an understanding of how people make decisions. To help this process, the Team's strategy has been to highlight the potential of certain interventions with robust analysis, however until these are taken

---

43 As part of the litter reduction campaign, actors were hired to perform ostentatious acts in the street and Fixed Penalty Notices of £75 for littering were displayed, both based on the idea of salience. Although the results were not statistically measured, this initiative won the Cleaner Safer Greener Network Innovation prize in 2010.

up on a large scale by the department in question they will remain as isolated good stories. In some cases. As has been highlighted in some areas, such as health and energy, departments are already setting up behavioural teams and allocating resources to integrate a behavioural approach into their work, which is a sign that the approach is becoming embedded.

Figure 17. London Boroughs' Direct Debit Prize Draw

Seventeen London Boroughs are participating in a scheme to make it easier for residents to pay their council tax, through direct debit. The scheme was launched in 2011 with a prize draw of £25,000 which attracted 34,500 new direct debit payers, which implied efficiency savings of £345,000 (£10 per person). The initial investment in the prize draw was recovered in 3 months.

Innovation type

The work of the Behavioural Insights Team draws on academic research that was pioneered in the 1960s by academics such as Daniel Kahneman, Richard Thaler and other US-based academics. While the concepts are not new – how psychology and behavioural science can help us better understand why people make certain apparently irrational economic decisions – the application of this field to public policy is innovative. The Behavioural Insights Team has two particularly innovative characteristics: first, taking insights from behavioural science and applying them to public policy; and, second, the trial-based methodology it has deployed.

Streamlined approach

Before the Team was set up, the Government's Science and Technology Select Committee produced a report on Behaviour Change, which recommended that the current mechanisms for sharing knowledge about behaviour change among government departments be reviewed with a view to introducing a more streamlined structure (Cabinet Office 2009). This has been one of the Behavioural Insights Team's tasks and to achieve this it has been given personal backing both by the Prime Minister and the Head of the Civil Service who chairs the Steering Group. While there is a host of isolated examples of applying behavioural science to public policy in different countries, before 2010 no government had set up team to rigorously identify opportunities for behavioural applications across government. As highlighted in the MINDSPACE review of previous work in this field, the examples cited are not connected by an overarching strategy, nor were they sufficiently trialled or implemented at scale. The Behavioural Insights Team has been given high-level support and leadership to tackle this new challenge.

Robust methodology

The trials-based approach to test the effectiveness of particular interventions has already been highlighted as the most innovative element of the Team's work (Service, Owain). The hallmark of the Team has been that, if it can be demonstrated that something works, with robust evidence-based data, then it is more likely that its uptake can be secured. Traditionally governments test different policy interventions with a pilot project, short-term trials or focus groups. However, these mechanisms cannot show whether the intervention has made a difference. While there may be some departments that claim that their policy design process is evidence-based and that they have used social scientists in the process, the application of Randomised Control Trials has not been systematically applied across the policy landscape. The policy process usually happens very quickly from pilot to roll-out and there is often a reluctance to have a sustained period of evaluation, as politicians are keen to have programmes up and running in a short period of time.

Trials also serve another purpose. The idea of government intervention to change people's behaviour is controversial and has received criticism from certain academics (Jones 2011). It is therefore important that behavioural interventions draw on hard evidence, so that the position can be explained in a rational way (Cabinet Office 2010). Effective evaluation should be considered at the beginning of the policy process, based not on outputs but outcomes, which should be established at the beginning of the process. Such evaluation should be sufficiently long-term that the intervention can result in maintaining behaviour change, ideally with a mix of pilot studies and controlled trials.

> «Introducing Randomised Controlled Trials in policy-making enables us to test the effectiveness of often subtle changes to policy so that we can identify what works. Very often these trials are developed in collaboration with academic advisors and will be based on insights from behavioural economics or psychology.»
> **—Owain Service,** Deputy Director of Behavioural Insights Team

Scalability and replicability

It is already apparent in the work that has been carried out that there is great potential for scaling up the Team's approach to finding innovative and cost-effective ways to change people's behaviour in order to meet certain environmental, social and economic policy objectives. The Team was initially charged with influencing two major areas of policy and has already successfully applied behavioural insights into the multiple areas discussed above, including organ donation, healthier food, consumer empowerment, tax and the environment. It is planning to extend activity to other areas such as mobile phone theft, smoking, higher education and the red tape challenge (reducing unnecessary regulation and replacing it with more effective alternative mechanisms).

It is useful to explore the conditions under which the Team was set up, which if they apply, may increase the chances of its being replicated successfully elsewhere (Table 26).

Table 26. Conditions for a successful government behavioural unit

CONDITION	DETAILS
High-level buy-in	The Steering Group is chaired by the Head of the Civil Service, and the Prime Minister has given the initiative his personal backing.
Behavioural expertise	A group of UK and international academics including Richard Thaler advise the team (Academic Advisory Board).
Competency mix	The team is made up of behavioural scientists as well as experienced policy-makers.
Demonstrating results	Sharing concrete results based on rigorous methodology has been an essential element of the Team's success in convincing government departments.
Initial funding	The team has been given an initial budget of £520,000 per year for two years.
Review mechanism	After the first two years the Team will be reviewed on its objectives, after which it will be easier to assess replicability.
Social science culture	Previous culture of social science in policy-making and use of evidence-based research. A review of behavioural work undertaken before setting up the team.
Leadership	David Halpern, expert in behavioural economics and former advisor to the Prime Minister is on secondment to lead the team.

Source: Compiled by authors

It is important to note, however, that, even if the above conditions are in place, behavioural economics is not always popular. Firstly, because people do not like to feel that they are part of an experiment and, secondly, governments who adopt it are open to the criticism of conceiving social problems as psychological pathology rather than admitting policy failure – particularly in the realms of public health and lifestyle-related issues. Naming the team "Behavioural Insights" rather than "Behavioural Change" was a conscious decision to prevent possible public criticism of the approach (Dr Peter John, Academic Advisory Board).

The US and France have also started work in applying behavioural economics to policy-making through the US Regulatory Affairs Unit in the US and the work of neuroscientist Oliver Oullier in France. It will be interesting to observe how behavioural economics can be applied in different cultural and socio-economic contexts.

———

Appendix 1. Further insights for reducing debt, error and fraud

Box 5. Making it easier to complete forms

A 2009 benchmarking study of tax administrations in 13 countries found that "most high performers tend to pre-populate all the fields for individuals' tax forms... thereby helping tax payers improve the accuracy of their submissions by ensuring that the forms are correct from the beginning".

A US study compared the effect of providing assistance in conjunction with a more streamlined process to complete the Free Application for Federal Student Aid (including pre-populating the form with information already held and help with completing the rest of the form) against simply providing information about the application process. The additional assistance and streamlined process substantially increased submissions and ultimately the likelihood of college attendance, persistence and aid receipt. College enrolment rates for high school seniors rose by eight percentage points (from 34% to 42%) in the year following the experiment. In contrast, the group that was only given information showed no significant difference from the control group, who received no information or support.

Behavioural Insights Team 2012

Box 6. Smartphone tax apps

The Inland Revenue Service in the United States has recently created a free smartphone app that allows taxpayers to check the status of their tax refund and obtain tax tips. Similarly, the Australian Tax Office has developed an easy-to-use tax calculator app that helps people to better understand how much personal tax they will pay on their earnings, as well as a Tax Receipt Log app. This app makes it easier to keep up to date on expenses and tax receipts by using the phone camera to take a photo of a receipt, which is then processed and stored. When it comes to the end of the financial year, the information can be simply emailed through, reducing the need to hunt for through piles of paper, search through credit card statements and manually calculate figures.

Behavioural Insights Team 2012

———

Appendix 2. Further insights on better presentation of information

Box 7. The personal touch

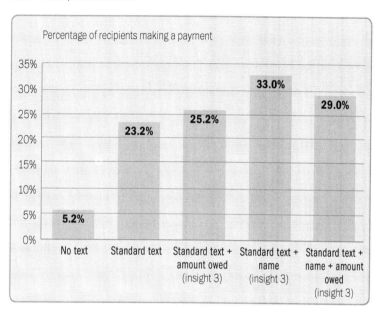

The statistics reflect the rates of response to text messages (in other words, when HMCTS had the correct mobile telephone number).

Behavioural Insights Team 2012 (a)

An experiment from the US tested the impact of Post-it notes and handwriting on people's likelihood of completing a survey. The survey, which was accompanied by a handwritten Post-it note requesting completion, received a 76% completion rate, compared with 48% when the handwritten message was on the cover page, which contained instructions about how to complete the survey, and 36% for those who received the survey and cover page only. In order to test whether it was the Post-it note itself that had the biggest impact, the researchers ran a similar experiment, in which a Post-it note with a handwritten note attracted a 69% response rate, compared with a 43% response to a blank Post-it note and 34% to no Post-it note. In addition, those who responded to the handwritten Post-it note returned the survey more promptly and with more detailed answers. When the experimenter added his initials and a "thank you", response rates increased even further.

Appendix 3. Further insights for energy efficiency

Energy Performance Certificates (EPCs) have been redesigned to provide clearer and more salient information. The messages and graphs have been simplified and the direct cost savings from installing energy-efficiency measures are highlighted.

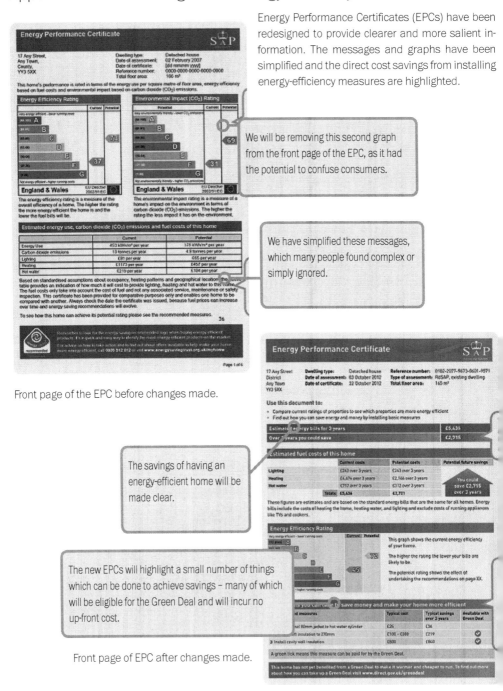

We will be removing this second graph from the front page of the EPC, as it had the potential to confuse consumers.

We have simplified these messages, which many people found complex or simply ignored.

Front page of the EPC before changes made.

The savings of having an energy-efficient home will be made clear.

The new EPCs will highlight a small number of things which can be done to achieve savings – many of which will be eligible for the Green Deal and will incur no up-front cost.

Front page of EPC after changes made.

———

Appendix 4. Further insights for health and social care

The Fureai Kippu scheme in Japan is a system whereby individuals can earn credits for looking after old people in their area in hourly units by helping with shopping, washing or other daily tasks. The credits can be saved for an individual's own use at a later stage or transferred to family members living in other parts of the country. There are now more than 400 branches in Japan with tens of thousands of participants.

Figure 18. Growth of Fureai Kippu branches

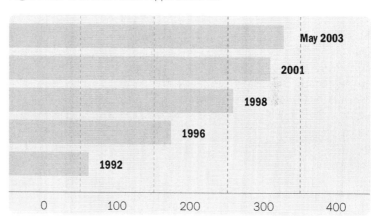

Source: B. Lietaer (2004) Complementary currencies in Japan today: Their history, originality and relevance. International Journal of Community Currency Research B: 1-23.

Figure 19. Fureai Kippu vouchers

———

References

AG Barr (2007)
Annual Report 20007

Ariely (2008)
Predictably Irrational

Behavioural Insights Team (2011)
Better Choices: Better Deals (Consumers Powering Growth)
Department for Business, Innovation and Skills and Behavioural Insights Team

Behavioural Insights Team (2010)
Applying Behavioural Insight to Health

Behavioural Insights Team (2011)
Behavioural Insights Team Annual update 2010–11

Behavioural Insights Team (2012) (a)
Applying Behavioural Insight to Reduce Fraud, Error and Debt

Behavioural Insights Team (2012) (b)
Test, Learn, Adapt: Developing Public Policy with Randomised Control Trials

Belsky and Gilovich (1999)
Why Smart People Make Big Money Mistakes ... and How to Correct Them

Bullock and Jones (2004)
Acceptable Behavioural Contracts Addressing Anti-social Behaviour in the London Borough of Islington.
Home Office online report.

Cabinet Office
www.cabinetoffice.gov.uk accessed on 15th December 2011

Cabinet Office (2009)
Government Response to the Science and Technology Select Committee Report on Behaviour Change

Department of Energy and Climate Change (2010)
Behaviour Change and Energy Use
Department of Energy & Climate Change, Behavioural Insights Team and Communities and Local Government

DWP (2011)
Guidance for Offering a Default Option for Defined Contribution Automatic Enrolment Pension Schemes.
Department for Work and Pensions

Gine, Karlan & Zinman (2008)
Put Your Money where Your Butt Is: A Commitment Contract for Smoking Cessation.
World Bank

Home Affairs Select Committee (2009)
Knife Crime

Institute for Government (2009)
MINDSPACE. Influencing Behaviour through Public Policy
Institute for Government & Cabinet Office

Jones et al. (2011)
Governing Temptation: Changing Behaviour in an Age of Libertarian Paternalism.
Aberystwyth University

New Economics Foundation (2005)
Behavioural Economics: Seven Principles for Policy Makers
Organ Donation Taskforce (2008)
The Potential Impact of an Opt Out System for Organ Donation in the UK
Prime Ministers Strategy Unit (2004)
Personal Responsibility and Changing Behaviour: The State of Knowledge and its Implications for Public Policy.
Thaler and Sunstein (2008)
Nudge. Improving decisions about Health, Wealth and Happiness
Wanless (2004)
Securing Good Health for the Whole Population: Final report – February 2004
Wansink and Kim (2006)
Bad Popcorn in Big Buckets: Portion size can Influence intake as much as taste.
Journal of Nutrition and Behaviour 37 (5): 242-245

Barcelona Exchange Networks[44]

A social movement based on motivating and involving people in the revival of the social bonds that foster mutual assistance and the reuse of goods for minor domestic and personal needs without having to use money as a medium of exchange.

Mission	Generate in the urban environment spaces for the exchange of goods and knowledge and networks for mutual assistance independent of financial transactions.
Founded	1987: First Goods Exchange Network set up in Mieres (Girona) 1992: First Knowledge Exchange Networks in Barcelona
Scalability	Replicable model on a neighbourhood scale
Location	Barcelona
Funding	Self-sufficient, without the use of money
Social impact	Neighbourhood level
Open innovation	Yes
Innovation	Self-managed, self-sufficient, reviving collective links in urban spaces

Introduction

In the majority of Barcelona's neighbourhoods, exchange markets are organised. There is also a series of individual initiatives undertaken via web pages, which promote the exchange of all types of things, including houses, cars and knowledge.[45] Many – though by no means all – of these initiatives are promoted by Redes de Intercambio (Exchange Networks, hereafter EN), given that many of these are organised either by local government or district bodies, such as parishes, neighbourhood and cultural associations, etc.

While the essential activity of the ENs is the organisation of exchange markets, in their respective neighbourhoods, their *raison d'être* is not limited to this. The ENs represent a social movement that promotes a philosophy of reciprocity and increasingly extensive collective neighbourhood action, which is present in almost all of the city's neighbourhoods. These networks arise as spontaneous initiatives by people who decide to organise themselves in order to achieve an aim of meeting their daily needs without using money as a medium of exchange.

In the current economic crisis, exchange as an alternative form of access to goods or knowledge is gaining greater strength and significance. However, these networks do not set out to meet only concrete needs, but also to recover and strengthen the social links between members of a neighbourhood and the value of mutual assistance. ENs also undertake another form of social action. Through their activity they make a

---

44 This case study has been undertaken by Milagros Paseta with guidance from David Murillo.
45 See Table 27.

form of social statement through collective action. For many people, it represents a positive and constructive channelling of non-conformity with the current social system based on consumption and individualism.

Some of the ENs in Barcelona already have a long history behind them and a strong capacity to mobilise volunteer participation such as those of Nou Barris, Castelldefels or Xaingra in Gràcia. Others that are newer are gaining an increasing importance in their respective neighbourhoods, such as the Xarxantoni in the Barrio de Sant Antoni, as well as relatively recent ENs such as those in Marina, which is the Marina de Port neighbourhood, Trocasec in Poble-sec, and Sants.[46]

Types of Exchange Networks. The ENs may be classified into two broad groups.
- The *Redes de Intercambio de Bienes* (RIB, Goods Exchange Networks, hereafter GEN), through which principally domestic items are exchanged (clothes, furniture, books, toys, etc.).
- The *Redes de Intercambio de Conocimientos* (RIC, Knowledge Exchange Networks, hereafter KEN), through which members of a neighbourhood organise themselves to give and/or receive a specific form of knowledge (computing courses, languages, art, healthcare, etc.)

The origin of the ENs is very diverse. There are those begun by people linked to teaching activity, union work, responsible consumer networks, neighbourhood organisations, NGOs or alternative movements. In general, it may be said that the key to the formation of these networks is the role played by the leader or leaders, who are people with a high degree of social conviction and commitment. For an exchange network to establish itself and become part of the social fabric of a neighbourhood, it is essential that there is a leader or leaders prepared to dedicate their time to defining the foundations of a project and involving the members of the neighbourhood in it. To put it another way, they must be people with motivation and conviction of the value of reciprocity and mutual assistance.

Table 27. Exchange Networks, Barcelona

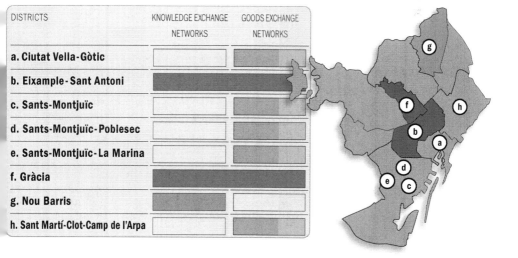

46 Representatives of the following networks have participated in this study: Nou Barris KEN, Xarxantoni GEN, La Marina GEN, Trocasec GEN, Sants GEN, and also the Castelldefels KEN. Three personal interviews were undertaken with Xavier Latorre of the Xarxantoni GEN, Xavier De Pedro of the La Marina GEN and Rafael Juncadella of the Nou Barris KEN. Four further questionnaire based interviews were undertaken with the Xarxantoni GEN, Trocasec GEN and the Sants GEN.

The origin of Barcelona's principal Exchange Networks

The paradigmatic GEN in Catalonia is that in Mieres (Girona), which has organised an annual market for 25 years. It began as a rural market, mainly with agricultural goods, but today visitors come from all over Catalonia and all types of goods are offered.

In Barcelona, the KEN considered as a pioneer and model is the Nou Barris KEN, which was formed at the beginning of the 1990s by teachers at the school for adults, the Freire de Nou Barris. They drew on their experience of the KEN run in Orly, which was founded 40 years ago and today extends across France. Currently, the KEN in Nou Barris is a key collective for social cohesion in the neighbourhood and delivers 15 daily workshops, on a range of themes, which are paid for exclusively through the exchange of other forms of knowledge or active collaboration in the network.

Another example is that of the Xaingra goods and knowledge EN in the neighbourhood of Gràcia, which has its origins in the efforts of a group of people linked to the anti-globalisation movement. This group, following a few pilot projects, decided to create the network in 2003 and it has been a notable success since then. Xaingra is based within the Ateneo Rosa de Foc, which is as umbrella organisation for other collective enterprises such as the consumer cooperative La Gleva, the food recycling group L'Olla Mòbil (The Mobile Saucepan), the consumer group Verduretes (Little Vegetables) and the theatre group Matraka. All of these are based on principles of assembly-based self-management, mutual assistance, green farming, self-training, anti-capitalism, action and critique, critical thought and solidarity.

Trocantoni is the GEN in the Sant Antoni neighbourhood. It was created in 2007 within the framework of the responsible consumerism commission Xarxantoni, which had set up an ecological consumer group in the neighbourhood.

Figure 20: Exchange market in the neighbourhoods of CollBlanc and la Torassa.

Photo: Wiros

Achievements and results

Although many of the ENs are still in the process of consolidation, they are increasingly achieving greater commitment and participation in the neighbourhoods in which they operate. There are neither verified statistics nor data on the level of impact, but in the opinion of those interviewed participation in the exchange markets is growing and more and more people attend out of an interest to get to know about their activity.

Goods exchanges

The organisation of the exchange markets is the principal activity of the GENs. The majority of these take place quarterly and coincide with the changes of season. The date and details of the organisation are decided at an assembly. However, each EN defines the finer points of the organisation in accordance with its own capacity and idiosyncrasy. The mechanism of the exchange markets is simple. There are two types of exchange offer: offers made by people who have a table on which they display their items; and the "visitors'" offers, made by those who attend the market with items to exchange with those on display. When someone finds something that interests them they negotiate with the owner to exchange it for something of theirs.

What happens when A is interested in something of B's, but B is not interested in anything A has to offer? As a philosophical principle of this type of market, the use of money as a medium for exchange is not permitted, so when situations like this arise, they can be resolved in a number of ways: by involving others in the exchange in such a way that each party gets something they want, or agreeing to a payment with food products (oil, flour, biscuits), or, in some cases, payment is made with self-produced handicraft products, which is something that the ENs have begun to strongly encourage.[47]

Currently, "payment" is one of the points that different ENs are evaluating in order to improve the mechanics and enhance the quality of exchanges. The possibility of developing a social currency that can be used as a medium of exchange is being considered, although, because of the complexity involved, this is at an early stage.[48]

Work is currently being undertaken on quality and dissemination, other aspects of the exchange markets requiring development. With regard to the quality of the goods offered, a large number of the table displays of items on offer is run by those considered "exchange professionals": people who do the rounds of various exchange markets and whose offer is of low quality. As far as promoting their activity is concerned the GENs are undergoing consolidation. They still have a lot of work to do on the dissemination and the production of information about their activities and to further their aim of attaining greater neighbourhood participation, not only in terms of users and those offering goods but also in the actual organisation of the Exchange Networks.

How the GENs function

The GENS generally organise themselves in the following way:
- Communication of the date and time to the networks' portal intercanvis.net
- Communication to the local council of the date and public space that they plan to use

---

47 Some GENS, such as Xarxantoni, have begun to "specialise" some of the exchange markets they organise; for example, last year in January after the Epiphany celebrations they organised a market specialised in toys for the first time.

48 In some neighbourhoods there is a social currency in circulation linked to cooperatives of organic producers. The most established is the ECO, managed by the Cooperativa Integral Catalana, which brings together nine Ecoxarxes [Eco networks] in Cataluña: http://cooperativaintegral.cat. For more information on social currencies see www.ces.org.za.

- Announcement to potential participants from the neighbourhood: the participants who want to offer goods must in some cases reserve their table either in advance or on the day at a time prior to the start of the event while the market is being set up.
- Dissemination and call for participation: preparation and distribution of explanatory material using posters at key points in the neighbourhood (shops, bars, libraries, civic centres and other public amenities), their own web pages or blogs, and social networks. The majority of those involved have an active presence in these types of networks.
- Setting up the market: this is often during the morning of the event. The majority are always held in the same public space
- Evaluation in the assembly meeting. The points that are evaluated are basically:
    - level of participation and origin of the visitors (from the neighbourhood or not)
    - origin of those offering goods (from the neighbourhood or not)
    - quality of the goods offered
    - user satisfaction

Only in a few cases is the evaluation conducted in a formal manner. It is generally based on the empirical evaluation of the organisation's members.

Knowledge exchanges

The Knowledge ENs function in a fairly distinctive manner. A person offers a specific form of knowledge (computing, cooking, painting, massage, a language, etc.) to a group of people that sign up to the workshop in question. At the same time these people must offer a form of knowledge in return, which the team organiser is in charge of channelling. For the KENs, "knowledge is the currency". Their philosophy is based on the idea that we can all learn something and we can all teach something independent of our economic, social or educational level.

The KENs, in contrast to the GENs, mobilise a number of people over a longer period of time and, as a result, the involvement is considerably greater. It is for this reason that the KENs, besides being knowledge exchange activities, generate other activities albeit more leisure-oriented ones such as fairs, excursions, etc. as well as creating a greater opportunity of forging bonds between the members of a neighbourhood and establishing the value of mutual assistance. Furthermore, as the KENs' users consist of a significant section of immigrants, they also facilitate the integration of this community into the neighbourhood and city.

For the KENs to function, it is fundamental that they can rely on a social leader, who can drive the enterprise forward, and a team of people who can organise and coordinate it on a permanent basis which is to say people with the will, commitment and time. It is for this reason that implementing a KEN involves considerable complexity. Some GENs have begun considering setting up knowledge exchanges too, but it is proving to be a difficult task; despite having tried in various formats, they have not managed to generate sufficient interest.

How the KENs function

To describe how the KENs work, we will focus mainly on the one run in Nou Barris, which is a long-running and very powerful network. There are four coordinating groups within the Nou Barris KEN: a group of ten people dedicated to the KEN's ongoing coordination, whose members have specific functions and meet on a monthly basis; the reception team, who deal with the people who approach the KEN for the first time and inform them about what they can study as well as offer; a third group links the aforementioned users with other small groups of users, depending on their areas of knowledge; and, finally, there are the network's members, who can participate in the three assemblies held each year in which generic issues and deeper concerns affecting the KEN are addressed.

To prepare for the beginning of each term, the ten members of the first group meet and organise the workshops to be undertaken: who will be the "knowledge facilitators" – as the workshop presenters are called – the number of places, the schedule and finally the distribution of information about the course, which is undertaken through the local civic centre, Ton i Guida, neighbourhood distribution channels and also the network's own blog.[49] However, according to their own members the main channel of dissemination is "word of mouth", given that the KEN is widely known in the neighbourhood. As well as using similar channels, the Castelldefels KEN uses social networks and its own list of email contacts.

Subsequently, the reception group sets to work on the "pairing-up": the balancing of what is received with what is offered. The level of management in a KEN depends on its size. For example, the Nou Barris KEN delivers 15 daily workshops all week for three-month terms and around 450 people take part annually. This enormous level of activity demands an equally significant level of involvement from the promotional group, which in this case is formed from ten volunteers.

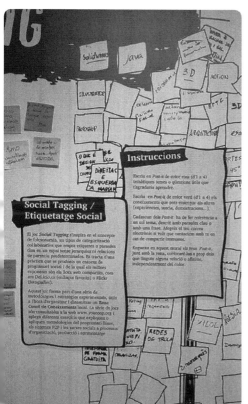

All the KENs have to have a space where they can deliver the workshops and undertake the related promotional activities. In the case of Nou Barris, the neighbourhood's council has granted them the use of the Ton i Guida Civic Centre. They carry out their activities there alongside the fee-charging workshops offered by the municipality in their own civic centre.

Figure 21. Knowledge Exchange Board in Girona

Photo: Bolit Centre d'Art Contemporani de Girona

Virtual exchange

In addition to the periodic exchange markets, it is also possible to make exchanges virtually, using, for instance, the portal Intercanvis.net. This portal was created in 2007 initially for Xaingra with the aim of creating a permanent environment for exchanges, rather than being limited to the face-to-face opportunities of the markets. In 2010, after several years functioning it was converted into the space for exchange for all the ENs in Catalonia and practically all of them signed up. Subsequently, to meet new needs the portal now also functions as a coordinating framework through the use of a shared calendar and an updated directory of the Catalan ENs. Intercanvis.net uses open-source software, which enables each EN to directly update its own information. It is currently open to all those users interested in offering goods or taking up offers, and it has more than 1,500 people registered.

The portal offers the possibility of receiving an e-bulletin with the different offers being registered organised according to users' interests and arranged by categories of specific goods, neighbourhood of origin, etc. There is also the option to sign up for a periodic bulletin and receive news and information about the activities run by the different ENs. In addition to this some ENs have their own virtual exchange channels. For Example, Xaingra (Gràcia) uses an email list with approximately 1,500 contacts to which they periodically send offers.

Impact and degree of transformation

The significance of the ENs goes beyond the exchange of goods and knowledge. The interest they generate, which makes them a valuable case study for social innovation, is based on their capacity to open a series of gateways to social transformation.

Different types of results

Currently, the types of impact they have may be considered as very disparate as it depends on the level of each EN's consolidation. For example, the more recent ones such as Trocasec or Marina are still endeavouring to make themselves known and integrate themselves into the fabric of their neighbourhoods, their community and associations. As a result, they place a marked emphasis on raising awareness of the values underpinning their initiatives: the satisfaction of daily needs without money and the mutual assistance of members of the neighbourhood.

The Xarxantoni, in the Sant Antoni neighbourhood, which has been functioning for some years, continues its promotional work, but the exchange markets are beginning to be a valid alternative means to satisfy people's daily needs. Furthermore, Xarxantoni has links to other initiatives such as "Millor que Nou" [Better than new],[50] which promote the use of goods until the end of their useful life, as well as repairing items rather than disposing of them. In this way the range of possibilities for sustainable and responsible consumerism is extended. Currently, this EN has as its next aim the implementation of a Knowledge Exchange Network, but it recognises that the involvement of the neighbourhood's members is not yet sufficient be able to set up an appealing and systematic set of knowledge exchange workshops.

The oldest networks studied, such as the Xaingra GEN in the Gràcia neighbourhood and the KEN in Nou Barris, are by now sufficiently advanced to be able to offer real alternatives to meet people's needs, and

---

50 The *Millor que Nou* (Better than new) campaign forms part of the *Programa metropolitano de gestión de residuos municipales* (PMGRM, Metropolitan programme for municipal refuse management) run by the Área Metropolitana de Barcelona's AMB (Metropolitan Area of Barcelona) Action programme.

as such, their impact on the social fabric of their respective neighbourhoods has likewise been sustained. Xaingra's seasonal exchange markets are well known to the members of the Gràcia neighbourhood, and the breadth of their offer and demand has contributed to the improvement of the quality of the items on offer. They have more than 1,500 people signed up to their email list and these individuals can organise exchanges through an e-bulletin. For many people from the Gràcia neighbourhood, Xaingra represents the possibility of obtaining goods without using money. Xaingra is also in a process of implementing a knowledge network in the neighbourhood.

The Nou Barris KEN, with almost 20 years behind, has become a model for the rest of the networks. Approximately 450 people annually benefit from the free workshops members of the neighbourhood offer in exchange for other types of knowledge. However, its social impact goes much further, as it fulfils a fundamental role in the neighbourhood: it facilitates social cohesion among neighbours, serves as one of the major sources of references and models for mutual assistance in the neighbourhood and it enables the integration of immigrants.

The Castelldefels KEN is also worthy of note as it has become a very powerful collective for neighbourhood initiatives. It is based on the values of mutual assistance, socialisation of knowledge, sustainable economy and integral education. It has more than 500 members, who, besides taking part in workshops, participate in leisure activities, solidarity campaigns, exchange markets for goods and a range of other periodic projects.

It is evident that the ENs have a major capacity to bring together a wide range of people irrespective of their economic or social status. The ENs have awoken different motivations among their users which, in turn, lead them to respond to the ENs' calls for action. We can define this as follows:

Box 8. Motivations for participation in the networks

Exchange Networks
- Find something that you need that you cannot or do not wish to buy
- Passing on useful things that you will not use
- Meet and spend time with other members of the neighbourhood
- Satisfy curiosity about the initiative, and, without having anything specific in mind, see if something of interest may be found

Knowledge Networks*
- Meet a concrete need to acquire a type of knowledge (for those who sign up)
- Create a sense of solidarity with members of the neighbourhood
- Establish relationships with members of the neighbourhood

* whether as user or "facilitator"[51]

In the case of both the KENs and the GENs, the common motivations are to satisfy a concrete need without using money as medium of exchange, and, which is of equal importance, to establish social ties and/or offer mutual assistance to members of the neighbourhood. Some of the people interviewed went so far as to emphasise that, for many people in the neighbourhood, above all the elderly and immigrants, the ENs served as way of avoiding isolation. There is therefore no doubt that the KENs, as a social collective format, have a major potential to achieve increasing social impact and contribute to a sense of community and the revival of

---

[51] "Knowledge facilitator" is how the Nou Barris KEN refers to those that deliver the workshops.

the value of mutual assistance, which, as they themselves underscore, has been gradually lost through the prevalent individualism of the current social system.

A constructive social movement: promoting social values and praxis

The ENs represent a social movement. Although, they do not define themselves as such and each unit has its own idiosyncrasies, it is a coordinated social movement which shares values, aims and know-how, as well as being completely open to taking in new groups interested in taking part. It is a movement that confronts individualism and seeks to revive the social ties and values that have become diluted in the urban environment: these are the relationship between the members of the neighbourhood, mutual assistance, and the notion of the "neighbourhood" as a community.

ENs also demonstrate the possibility of social initiatives being carried out in a self-managed way by the members of a neighbourhood themselves.[52] Put another way, they offer a way for community members to organise themselves to resolve community affairs without the need to involve any public entity. In this sense, the ENs are a model of organisation that offers the members of a neighbourhood and the city a simple and gratifying form of citizen participation. A key factor is that it requires a very low level of commitment and provides the possibility of a concrete recompense.

Another innovative aspect to be highlighted is that ENs demonstrate a form of promoting social values taken to a level of praxis, which is far cry from the "all talk and no action" of some groups. The thinking of the ENs is advancing in a slow but steady way. Through the example offered by their activities, the exchange markets and knowledge exchange workshops, they work directly with the social fabric of the neighbourhood by teaching concepts such as responsible consumerism, sustainability, self-management, citizen participation, etc. In this sense, the ENs represent a simple "format" for social communication, based on the idea that we all have something to give and receive, something to learn and something to teach.

In a similar vein, it may be added that the ENs also represent an alternative form of socially responsibility among members of a neighbourhood. They offer a form of direct and reciprocal solidarity. It is not only about giving, but also receiving.

The value of material things and knowledge

At the core of the ENs' philosophy is the fact that the value of material things and knowledge are not measured by money. Material things are valued according to the worth they have for the people who give and receive them. A leather jacket, for instance, could be worth two kilos of flour and a few second-hand books or an hour-long Arabic conversation class. For the ENs, the value of what is exchanged is always relative and is decided on by the two parties who negotiate the exchange.

For example, it could be that A has an old radio that they need to get out of the house immediately and are prepared to exchange it for a slice of cake. At the same time, it may be that, for B, the same radio has great value because it reminds them of one their grandfather had at home. In a similar manner, the knowledge about a specific type of massage a qualified masseuse teaches in a KEN might have the same value as the knowledge imparted by a woman with no qualification who teaches Caribbean cookery.

A virtual environment for exchange

Another of their innovative aspects is the intercanvis.net platform mentioned above. This is a virtual tool

---

52 In this sense in the majority of the neighbourhoods in Barcelona there are also organic and locally sources products consumer cooperatives. The ENs are an open organisation model – assembly-based – that has begun to operate and implies a new approach to self-sustenance and community action.

that allows for exchanges and enables relationships in a permanent manner, not only at a neighbourhood level, but across the city and the region of Catalonia. In this way, it offers a point of entry for those who are interested in setting up a new exchange network and sharing the collective's values. Furthermore, the ENs are formed with a more or less explicit vocation for social change and promote a change of perception and attitude about the following issues:

- Community life, focused on strengthening the social bonds between neighbours: a more human, closer and more reciprocal relationship.
- More responsible forms of consumerism
- Environmental sustainability, changing attitudes towards reuse and recycling
- A more active collective participation in or "belonging" to a community

It would seem that, in the case of some ENs, there is still a great deal of work to be done to convert themselves into real means of meeting social needs. Among their greatest challenges is the increase of the quality of the objects offered and attaining an increased commitment from the members of the neighbourhoods to consolidate the knowledge ENs. Nonetheless, laying the foundations of restoring to society the possibility of relating to one another in a collective form and helping one another in a mutual form is a notable endeavour, above all in the current crisis.

Collaboration across different sectors

Although each EN in Barcelona is independent in terms of management, there is an overarching coordination framework called InterXarxes,[53] which convenes the periodic assemblies of the different networks. These assemblies coordinate the different events that the ENs organise to avoid any overlapping of events, as well as allowing them to share experiences and views. They also seek to make progress on other communal issues such as the creation of a common social currency to facilitate exchange, forms of sustainability and the replicability of the model. The ENs that belong to the InterXarxes, share a series of aims and values that underpin their activity:

Box 9. Characteristics of the ENs

Common aims
- Strengthen the social bonds between the members of their respective neighbourhoods, as well as promote values of confidence, mutual assistance, reciprocity and solidarity to address daily needs
- Facilitate the reuse of goods to promote sustainability and to oppose unbridled consumerism
- Promote and organise exchanges between individuals or groups of both knowledge and goods
- Provide education about values related to other forms of consumerism, social relations and active citizen participation
- Raise people's self-esteem, reinforce the idea that we all have something to give and receive, to teach and to learn

Share values
- Principle of mutual assistance among members of a neighbourhood: oppose individualism by forging personal ties and reviving other forms of meeting needs without the use of money
- Consumerism based on responsibility: re-learning how to live according to responsible consumerism
- Environmental sustainability: reusing things instead of disposing of them in good condition
- Open practice: ENs are totally open and willing to share their experience
- Autonomous and self-sufficient: this enables them to be independent and be able to act with total freedom, without having to depend on public administrations, or any other type of external entity

---

53 Translation: Internetworks.

Relationship with the public administration

In general, local administrations, both at a neighbourhood level and that of the city of Barcelona, support the EN initiatives as, directly or indirectly, they facilitate their own activity. In this sense, the use of public space, with a request made beforehand, is guaranteed as well as promotion of the ENs' activities though local channels. There is also an interest in creating synergies between the GENs and Barcelona Council's aforementioned campaign *Millor que Nou*, which collaborates with some ENs by granting them equipment for the exchange markets (partitions, seats, second-hand or restored tables) and sharing a date and space for the undertaking of their activities as in the case of Xarxantoni.

In other cases, such as the Nou Barris KEN, the local council has allowed them to use the facilities in the Ton i Guida civic centre for their workshops. The space is used by many of the neighbourhood's other groups and associations and it is worth noting that, apart from the specific municipally funded workshops, the Nou Barris KEN is that which generates the most activity and attendance.

In addition to this, there are some examples of the ENs' being given annual grants to fund their activity (between €1,500 and €3,000 depending on the council). In other cases, such as Xarxantoni, they receive a grant from Barcelona Council's *Área de Medioambiente* (Environment Division).

The interest that the ENs have awoken in local administrations is reflected in the publication entitled *Guía Barcelona per l'acció comunitaria. Xarxes de Intercanvi Solidari* (Barcelona Guide for community action. Solidarity Exchange Networks),[54] which was published in December 2009 by Barcelona Council's Institut de Govern i Polítiques Públiques (Institute of Governance and Public Policies), which belongs to the Área de Participación y Movimientos Sociales (Social Participation and Movement Division). This guide compiles research on the existing ENs in Barcelona up to the date of publication, in addition to the different neighbourhoods' range of organic farming consumer cooperatives and time banks: in other words, all the initiatives that are identified as solidarity exchange activities.

However, it is important to highlight that, in principle, the ENs are not interested in establishing a deeper relationship with the local administrations, since they want to maintain their level of self-sufficiency, autonomy and self-management.

Economic sustainability and long-term viability

All the ENs in Barcelona are self-sufficient. Their operating costs are very low and the majority are able to cover their economic expenditure in a range of ways that will be discussed in this section.

Personnel team

In every case everyone who collaborates in the network's activities and organisation does so on a voluntary basis. As a result, the ENs define the activities to be undertaken with regard to the available hours of volunteering.

In the majority of cases, the networks have a more or less stable team of people that functions as an incentivising force. This team is often that which participates in the monthly coordination meetings and the more occasional InterXarxes general assemblies. They also work on the organisation of the tasks that

---

54 The guide may be consulted at: http://w3.bcn.es/fitxers/observatorisocial/xarxesintercanvi.270.pdf.

require their input, whether it be the organisation of the exchange markets, knowledge exchange workshops or occasional leisure activities.

In the case of the KENs, the level of involvement of the collaborators is very high as the organisation and monitoring of the workshops demands a major permanent effort. In the case of the GENs the workload is considerably less.

Equipment

In terms of the equipment required, in the case of the GENs, Barcelona Council's Millor que Nou programme provides all the necessary material to hold the exchange markets (seats, tables, partitions), which is shared by the ENs that require them, such as Xarxantoni, Trocasec and La Marina. In other examples, such as Xaingra or Sants, the EN asks the participants to provide their own display materials. In the case of the KENs, those attending the workshops take responsibility for their own material.

Workspaces

In so far as the use of workspaces is concerned, all the ENs have their own, which may be for their exclusive use or shared with other neighbourhood associations. Some ENs, such as Xarxantoni, have a workspace granted to them by the council for a limited time. For the GENs a workspace is necessary in order to meet, store materials for the markets and to serve as a point of reference for people interested in participating.

For the KENs, it is fundamental to have a workspace as they need a permanent venue to deliver their knowledge exchange workshops. These spaces are often granted by their district centre or council. For example, the Nou Barris KEN uses the Ton i Guida civic centre's facilities and the Castelldefels KEN has a workspace provided by the council.

Grants

In some cases, such as Trocantoni, Nou Barris and Trocasec, although only at the outset of its work, the ENs receive an annual grant from their district councils that ranges from €1,500 to €3,000 for running costs and which allows them to cover their office and publicity costs. However, receipt or not of this type of money from the public administration depends on each networks' character and attitude. Networks such as Xaingra or Sants, hold to a principle of not receiving any type of grant, as they consider this a way to assure their absolute self-sustainability and freedom to act. It should be noted that Xaingra was begun as an anti-globalisation movement, which is characterised by being alternative and critical of the current socio-economic system.

Grants from private entities

There has been no collaboration between the networks and the private sector. However, local businesses are often willing to offer discounts for photocopies or cover electricity expenses for an activity linked to an exchange market.

There is only one case, that of the Nou Barris KEN, in which this form of collaboration has been especially relevant. The enormous volume of its activities led to an increase of certain running costs (telephone and office expenses), which led to them receiving their first donation in 2011: €3,000 from a nearby branch of la Caixa bank intended to cover those costs. However, as noted, this issue is at the discretion of each network.

Promotional media and office resources

In general, all the promotional media that the ENs use are free, whether their own, as a rule virtual ones (web pages, blogs, email lists, Facebook, etc.), or those that they can use for free such as local or neighbourhood media, etc. The implementation and maintenance of the virtual promotional media is often undertaken by the members of the organisation or other volunteers. They also take responsibility for the graphic design of the publicity materials that are placed in neighbourhood shops and other important public spaces (libraries, civic centres, etc.). The printing costs of these materials and other office expenses are often covered by the network itself or by individual members of the organisation.

Figure 22: One "eco" – complementary currency used in Catalonia

InterXarxes portal: intercanvis.net

The portal shared by Catalonia's ENs, intercanvis.net, is an important and very useful multi-managed and self-sustainable tool that has been developed and maintained by volunteers. Its contents are registered under a Creative Commons licence,[55] and it uses technology that allows each EN to sign up, and use a space to present itself and promote its activities. Each EN manages its own content and can access the shared schedules of the ENs, publish news and announcements, etc.

On the other hand, those interested in exchanging material things or knowledge, having signed up to the portal, can publish their offers and access all the other offers in a simple way. At present, this fulfils three main aims: enabling exchanges between users, the promotion of the ENs' activities and coordination between the individual networks.

Type of innovation

In all the cases studied, there is a positive attitude towards transmitting their activity to other neighbourhoods when interest is shown and is sought after. In fact the EN network InterXarxes, which holds assembly periodically, also enables the exchange of views about experiences to contribute to the improvement of each EN's functioning.

---

55 For more information see: http://creativecommons.org/licenses/by-sa/3.0/deed.ca.

It is worth highlighting that one of the aims set out in the last InterXarxes assembly, in December 2011, was to develop the intercanvis.net portal as a tool to facilitate the creation of new networks in different neighbourhoods, whenever there is interest to do so, by providing an updated directory of all the ENs, with references and contact details. In this way, the ENs make themselves available to collaborate with others who are keen to create a network.

The intercanvis.net portal is also a self-managed tool, which is to say that all the registered networks can modify content, and the person who created and maintains it is a volunteer whose intention is to share this role so that the portal can continue to provide a self-sustainable tool for the network.

Promotional team

The creation and implementation of a new EN arises from an individual's or a group of neighbourhood residents' interest in dedicating part of their time to an activity that will improve their community. In the majority of cases, these people contact the ENs they most identify with or that are best known or most established; they are always available to share their know-how and facilitate the process.

In the event that they decide to undertake the project, they can sign up to the intercanvis.net portal, attend the InterXarxes coordination assemblies and publish and promote their activities sin the shared calendar of events.

With regard to organisation, the majority of the ENs in Barcelona have followed the internal organisation model used by the Nou Barris KEN, which has played the role of pioneer and model for all the others. Although each EN adapts this model of organisation to suit their particular characteristics, it basically consists of:

- An assembly-based organisation, with periodic calls to meetings open to all members of the neighbourhood
- A voluntary "promotional" team that meets on a monthly basis to coordinate and take decisions about the EN and its activity
- A way of working based on values of self-management and active participation, and depending on the commitment of people who undertake both new and established activities

A spontaneous evolution process

Bearing in mind the difficulty of obtaining the involvement of members of the neighbourhood, in every case there is a group of people that act on a more or less continual basis to incentivise others. Their members, who are all volunteers, have established roles for the functioning of the EN (accounts, authorisation management, activity dissemination, assembly organisation, participant motivation, etc.).

Working from this foundation, each EN defines its activities, its schedule, its promotional channels and the type of relationship that it wants to establish with its district council. On the basis of the commitment generated within the neighbourhood, each goes on to define its community identity and role. Some of them manage to become part of the neighbourhood's social fabric, while others become diluted and go no further than organising periodic events.

According to some of those interviewed, implementing an EN is not an easy task and it is not achieved overnight. Furthermore, it is much more than the organisation of an exchange market, as it demands commitment and a vision of the future based on a different form of citizen participation and community action. However, this does not mean that it is a rigid model of organisation as many periodic initiatives become ENs over time. In many cases, it is a question of a spontaneous evolutionary process.

Figure 23: Promotional material for a "Better than New" public recycling and goods exchange campaign

Photo: Civic centre, Sandaru Park[56]

Scalability and replicability

With regard to the model's scalability, slowly but surely over the last few years ENs have been created in almost all of the city's neighbourhoods as well as other locations in Catalonia. It may be argued that the EN as an innovative proposal for the creation of collective links is being widely taken up in Catalan society.

Their scalability is based on a spontaneous network model according to which the groups are organised in their respective neighbourhoods. It is relatively simple and the only other complication is the issues raised by specific, individual activities. Their potential is infinite, since all that is needed to set them up is the commitment from the team of people who want to organise and launch the EN. Nonetheless, in many cases it is precisely this commitment that is the most difficult to sustain.

However, the scale that individual instances of the model can achieve is limited. Basically, the problem is that their structure is based on limited groups of volunteers, who create networks at first with high motivation, but later meet with major difficulties when it comes to finding new members to commit themselves to the organisation in a consistent manner. The difficulty faced in achieving the renovation of the "core team" is the major stumbling block for their growth and a significant risk for their long-term survival. In this sense, the task of educating the members of the neighbourhood about their work is fundamental for the ENs to achieve community involvement.

In terms of the replicability, in the case of the Goods Exchange Network as soon as the "core team" is organised and motivated the rest is simple. As has been shown, the oldest networks have provided support and a model for the new ones. As was the case with Nou Barris for Xaingra, Xaingra and Nou Barris for Trocantoni and then Trocantoni for Trocasec and Sants. Nou Barris effectively set the organisational template, as their activity of the others is different. This template basically consists of a more or less stable promotional team that meets periodically to take decisions about the network to focus it on their aims and principles, organise and coordinate their activities and also relationships with other networks. Xaingra provided the model for the organisation of the exchange markets, although these all differ with regard to the relationship with the local administration. For example, Xaingra and Trocasec "inform" the administration that they will use a specific public space, while the others ask for permission.

The Knowledge Exchange Network is very different. Some KENs, like Trocantoni, Xaingra and Trocasec, are trying to replicate the Nou Barris model, but it is proving very difficult to achieve the commitment that the organisation and coordination requires, as well as the level of involvement of those who would be their actual users, the members of the neighbourhood. This is one of the important challenges that the KENs seek to overcome in the future.

Principal challenges for replicating

The principal challenges currently facing the ENs with regard to replicability are the following:

For the GENs

- Ensuring the renewal of their core teams in order to ensure the sustainability of the EN and to avoid its dependence on the individuals that helped launch or lead the network.
- Increasing the level of involvement from members of the neighbourhood, increasing the ratio of tables of items on offer from the neighbourhood and reducing the number of so-called "exchange professionals".
- Increasing the amount of handcraft "home-made" products as a medium of exchange, as well as second-hand goods.
- Finding a way to adapt the model of existing KENs and including knowledge exchange in their neighbourhoods. Until now, many of the GENs have tried a range of ways that have not proved successful for two reasons: a significant amount of time is required from the volunteers and no way of promoting the project has been found that inspires sufficient interest or commitment from members of the neighbourhood.

For the KENs

- The workshop users need to give back their knowledge to the network on their own initiative, as in many cases the members of the core team have to send out reminders to them. Essentially, the user must understand the basic points of the KEN philosophy: "receive and give" and "we all have some knowledge to provide".
- Finding a better way of channelling new knowledge, as on the whole the workshops are repeated term after term, and this creates waiting lists of others who want to give new workshops, which in many cases never have the opportunity to be run.

———

References

Illacrua (2004)
Revista *Els Quaderns de Participacció,* No. 3. Associació Cultural Illacrua, January 2004.
Institut de Govern i Polítiques Públiques Bellaterra (2009)
Barcelona per l'acció comunitària. Xarxes d'intercanvi solidari. Àrea de Participació i moviments socials.

———

Appendix 1. Other exchange initiatives in Catalonia

Other exchange initiatives

www.trueQueweb.com / www.quierocambiarlo.com / www.intercanvis.org / www.segundamanita.com /
www.nolotiro.org / www.intercambiocasas.com / www.truequear.com / www.loquo.com /
www.facebook.com /lostandfoundworld / www.compartir.org / www.hitchhiker.org / www.bookcrossing.
com / www.red-bdt.org / www.sindinero.org / www.basurama.org/index.htm / www.sol-violette.fr

Knowledge exchange initiatives

Xaingra, the exchange network, la Vila de Gràcia, Barcelona: http://ateneurosadefoc.wordpress.com/about
The Nou Barris knowledge exchange network: http://xarxaintercanvidenoubarris.blogspot.com
XARCLOT, the knowledge exchange network Clot: xarclot@hotmail.com
The Collblanc knowledge exchange network: www.xic.cat
The Castelldefels knowledge exchange network: intercanvicastell@hotmail.com
The Girona knowledge exchange network: xicgirona@hotmail.com

Goods exchange initiatives

Mercat Escolar de l'Intercanvi Virtual: www.residus-altemporda.org/mercat-escolar/web
The Reus exchange network: www.reus.cat/medi_ambient/donocanvionecessito/links.php
The Centre Cívic de la Sagrada Família exchange market: padega7@yahoo.es
Exchange market, Sant Antoni, Barcelona: www.xarxantoni.net/Projecte%20Trocantoni
Communal knowledge bank: www.bancocomun.org
The Les Corts solidarity free service bank: www.bancsolidari.org

Other exchange initiatives in Catalonia

Vols Tens: www.barcelona.volstens.org
Lost and Found Barcelona: www.lostandfoundbcn.com
La Cooperativa Integral Catalana: http://cooperativaintegral.cat
The Catalonia exchange website: http://intercanvis.net/tiki-index.php
L'Ecoxarxa de Barcelona: https://barcelona.ecoxarxes.cat
Barcelona Actua: www.barcelonactua.org
Millor que Nou, 100% vell (Better than New, 100% old): http://millorquenou.blogspot.com

3

Review of social innovation concepts

The following section offers a survey of the latest concepts and thinking around social innovation developed by a selection of leading opinion-makers from academic centres and social innovation hubs around the world. We have organised this information around our five chosen variables, for each of which we present a selection of the most widely accepted concepts, models and frameworks and highlight some of the key authors and advocates of these models, as well as illustrate some practical examples of social innovation. We do not aspire to present an exhaustive literature review, but simply draw to out some useful definitions and frameworks for those interested in gaining a deeper understanding of how social innovation really works.

Research history

Public debate around social innovation has been going on for decades, however academic research has been slower on the uptake; by 2008 only 20 peer-reviewed articles with social innovation or social entre-preneurship in their title had been published. Reasons for this include the lack of journals for publishing articles on the subject, the limited availability of reliable data and overall low levels of interest in the academic sector for such an apparently diffuse subject (Nicholls 2009). In contrast, there has been more activity in teaching than research. According to a study by Ashoka 250 members of academic faculties were identified as teaching social innovation by 2007.

Three waves of academic activity have been identified. The first was kick-started by Austin and Dees. It was based on management theory and taken up across US business schools (1998–2001). The second wave of interest flourished in Europe and incorporated various social sciences perspectives. Considerable activity was undertaken by the Saïd Business School (2002–2007). Finally, the third wave (2008 onwards) has consisted of research activity that has spread to Asia, Australia and Africa. The understanding of social innovation has also shifted during these phases, from an initial view of it as a commercial activity delivering a public good to later development into a second conception concerned with delivering solutions to social problems using radically new models that promote systemic change (Nicholls 2009).

Definitions of social innovation

There are today many definitions of social innovation ranging from the simple *"new ideas (products, ser-ices and models) developed to fulfil unmet social needs"* (Bacon *et al.* 2008) to the more complex *"A novel solution to a social problem that is more effective, efficient, sustainable, or just than existing solutions and for which the value created accrues primarily to society as a whole rather than private individuals"* (Phills *et al.* 2008).[57] Three essential characteristics of social innovation can be distilled from all of the most cited definitions: first, the novelty and effectiveness of the idea; second, its orientation towards solving a social problem (encompassing social, environmental, economic and ethical challenges); and, finally, its generation of a social rather than individual value.

Many authors also note that social innovation can take diverse forms, it can be a product, a production process or a piece of technology. However, it can also be an idea, a principle, a piece of legislation, a social movement, an intervention or some combination of all of these. In fact, some of the best recognised social innovations are combinations of a number of these elements (Nicholls 2009, Phills *et al.* 2008). *"Innovation is often given complex definitions; we prefer the simple one, 'New ideas that work'."* (Mulgan *et al.* 2007).

There are a family of terms such as social entrepreneurship, social enterprise and social innovation that prompt considerable debate, although there is a general consensus that they refer to different aspects of this emerging sector. Social entrepreneurship is used to explore the personal qualities of the individuals starting up a particular initiative, such as leadership, radical thinking and the capacity to innovate and inspire others. Social enterprise is the term used to reflect the organisational model chosen to solve a particular social problem, with a focus on achieving the dual objective of economic and social value. Finally, social innovation is often seen as more far-reaching and radical, promoting systemic change.

In addition to the host of definitions, there is an abundance of tools and mechanisms to *stimulate* social innovation deployed by all types of social innovation hub, ranging from government agents, academic centres and the many foundations and organisations focused on generating more social innovation. Murray *et al.*'s "The Open Book of Social Innovation" provides a comprehensive directory of over 300 of these tools and mechanisms. However, despite the richness and vitality of the sector there is very little consensus about how to measure social innovation and how to define its social impact. There is also a striking lack of consistency in reporting metrics and methodologies. Inspired by the dynamism and diversity of thinking on social innovation, we have set out to tackle the diffuseness and lack of clarity that also often characterise it by defining a set of key variables to better understand the potential of any given social innovation. In the following pages we explore the thinking around each one of these chosen variables.

---

57 See Appendix 1 for further definitions of social innovation.

———

Key references

Dees, J.G. (1998)
The Meaning of "Social Entrepreneurship". Comments and Suggestions Contributed from the Social Entrepreneurship Founders Working Group.
Durham, NC: Center for the Advancement of Social Entrepreneurship, Fuqua School of Business, Duke University.

Mulgan, G., Tucker, S., Ali, R., & Sanders, B. (2007)
Social Innovation: What it is, why it matters and how it can be accelerated.
Oxford Saïd Business School, Skoll Centre for Entrepreneurship. London.

Murray, R., Caulier-Grice, J., & Mulgan, G. (2010)
The Open Book of Social Innovation.
The Young Foundation and NESTA.

Nicholls, A. (2008)
Social Entrepreneurship: New Models of Sustainable Social Change.
Paperback Edition, Oxford University Press.

Nicholls, A. (2009)
Learning to Walk: Social Entrepreneurship, Innovations.
Special Edition Skoll World Forum, pp. 209-222

Phills Jr., J.A., Deilglmeier, K., & Miller, D.T. (2008)
Rediscovering Social Innovation.
Stanford Social Innovation Review, Fall 2008.

Impact and degree
of social transformation

There is an increasing demand to measure social impact and the degree of social transformation from a range of stakeholders, particularly funders, investors and governments, as well as social entrepreneurs themselves. However, in practice many social innovations are unable to meet this demand. In this section we explore the question why measure social impact? To do so, we consider which aspects of social innovation can be measured and by highlighting some of the many mechanisms used, as well as some of the organisations innovating in this field, we discuss how this can be done.

There is a general consensus from the key authors on the subject about the strategic reasons for attempting to measure social impact. The first and perhaps most obvious is related to resource acquisition and being able to respond to the specific demand from funders and investors for data on impact. The tremendous growth in socially responsible investment across the world is a key factor here, as is indicated in the box below; increasingly, social innovations need to report on both their social and financial returns to funders and investors, regardless of whether they are private, public or groups of individuals.

Box 10. The rise of socially responsible investment (SRI)

In 2010, professionally managed assets in the US following SRI strategies stood at $3.07 trillion, a rise of more than 380% from the $639 billion in 1995, whereas across the same period a conventional use of assets rose only by 260%. More recently, since 2005, SRIs have seen a 34% growth whereas regular investment resulted in only a 4% rise. In 2010 1 in every $8 invested in the US is involved in SRI, and these investments can be classified in the following three ways: 1) environmental, social and governance investment analysis 2) shareholder activism and 3) the fastest-growing SRI sector, loans, investments and participation in social or community projects with alternative investment funds. The driving forces for this type of investment include the emerging market of environmental products and services, community investing, social impact investment, legislative and regulatory developments, new funding styles, social venture capital, triple bottom line private equity and responsible property funds.

Source: US Socially Responsible Investment Forum

The second strategic reason for measuring impact, as with any enterprise striving for effectiveness and efficiency, is to aid performance enhancement. Measuring progress against social objectives is commonly seen as a tool to help make more informed internal management decisions as well as to better understand the long-term processes of social change. While in this regard the pressure is less immediate than that from funders or regulators requiring an annual report, there is a trend being observed towards the greater professionalisation of the social sector with some leading social innovations demonstrating a level of efficiency and effectiveness more commonly recognised in the private sector.

The third reason for measuring impact has been described as organisational self-legitimisation. In other words, the drive to prove to the world that the organisation is making a difference, which is demonstrated explicitly by the example of the Furniture Resource Centre Group's[58] report "We Do Good Things, Don't We?" (Nicholls 2009). NGOs' social missions and non-profit status has engendered the systemic trust in them. However, the social mandate and number of supporters or members gives the organisation a "legitimacy surplus" and hence there is less demand on measuring and reporting on its activities, which leads to reduced public accountability and a lack of motivation for measurement. However, in the context of the current explosion of social enterprises and organisations with a social mission in order to maintain this sense of trust and legitimacy, as well as compete with similar organisations for the same funds, there is an increasing need to be able to demonstrate impact.

For social entrepreneurs and organisations with a social purpose aiming to innovate in the context of long-standing institutional and systemic failures, such as housing, education and access to credit, the conventional social impact reporting mechanisms are inadequate (Nicholls 2009).

What to measure?

There is a growing diversity of methods of social innovation "from Finnish Complaints Choirs to Korean Imagination Banks, from Italy's social enterprise bank to US venture philanthropy models, Danish public service laboratories to Brazilian participatory budgeting" (Murray et al. 2011). Given the breadth of the spectrum, the challenge of comparing one social innovation to another is huge. Consider for example the contrast of an electric vehicle system, which could be measured in terms of the reduction of carbon emissions, with a drug rehabilitation programme, which requires an individual qualitative assessment over time.

There is also growing debate concerning the different processes of social innovation; however, less has been said about which stage of the process should be measured. Financial accounting systems have been developed, established and even regulated over the last 100 years to inform public expenditure decision-making on the basis of quantitative analysis of performance and impact, and this has supported a trend for a more evidence-based policy. Unfortunately, the social sector has developed with limited common mechanisms for reporting, a wide disparity of indicators, and minimum regulation regarding disclosure of social impact.

An additional challenge is the difficulty in establishing relationships between different financial inputs (grants, donations, in-kind contributions, social capital, etc.) and actual social impact in "multiple, distinctive, non-comparable" outputs (Nicholls 2009).

A review of the different stages of the process of social innovation is one way to seek clarity about which aspect of social innovation is most relevant or useful to measure. At the most basic level, there are three stages; the development of the process or product, its dissemination and the social value created. All of these could be monitored and measured both with qualitative and quantitative indicators. Murray et al., in their compendium of tools and resources, describe six stages of social innovation as indicated in the box below. The authors note that these stages are not necessarily sequential. A social innovation may jump from idea to implementation directly and that there are also a series of feedback loops as innovations mature and adapt with time.

---

58 A leading UK social business giving people in unemployment and poverty the chance to change their lives: www.frcgroup.co.uk.

Box 11. Social Innovation Spiral

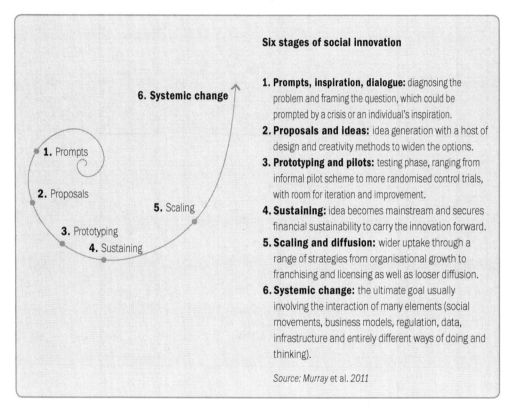

Six stages of social innovation

1. **Prompts, inspiration, dialogue:** diagnosing the problem and framing the question, which could be prompted by a crisis or an individual's inspiration.
2. **Proposals and ideas:** idea generation with a host of design and creativity methods to widen the options.
3. **Prototyping and pilots:** testing phase, ranging from informal pilot scheme to more randomised control trials, with room for iteration and improvement.
4. **Sustaining:** idea becomes mainstream and secures financial sustainability to carry the innovation forward.
5. **Scaling and diffusion:** wider uptake through a range of strategies from organisational growth to franchising and licensing as well as looser diffusion.
6. **Systemic change:** the ultimate goal usually involving the interaction of many elements (social movements, business models, regulation, data, infrastructure and entirely different ways of doing and thinking).

Source: Murray et al. 2011

As has been mentioned, there is a host of mechanisms to support social entrepreneurs or social enterprises at each stage of the process, and they have prompted a growing culture of measuring their effective uptake of social entrepreneurship. The first two stages, outlined above, are typically used in government-led participatory processes with a particular social goal, such as regenerating an urban landscape or improving local childcare provision. A host of quantitative indicators around the number of people involved is used in the dialogue phase; for example, the proposals developed and even their popularity are commonly used. Prototypes and pilots are also easy to measure on a superficial level; however, their real potential to sustain change is more difficult to identify. Randomised control testing is a more sophisticated tool that is starting to be used in some cases to test the potential of a pilot scheme in a more robust way.

The real challenge of what to measure lies in the last three stages of the cycle; sustaining, scaling and, above all, systemic change. These are particularly problematic when a social initiative sets out to solve a specific social problem, such as the reduction of water-borne diseases in a region, and ends up with a radical change of the whole system: for example, developing community financing models for local sanitation systems, as is the case of Gram Vikas.[59]

59 Gram Vikas is an NGO providing innovative relief and sanitation solutions across India since the 1970s: http://gramvikas.org.

How to measure?

Within welfare economics, it has been suggested that the value of a social good can be priced at what a beneficiary or consumer would be willing to pay for it (Nicholls 2009), which allows performance outputs to be compared with resource inputs. This methodology has also been commonly used in bio-diversity conservation – how much would individuals or communities be willing to pay to keep an area of land, or even a particular species, under protection? Existing protected areas of natural beauty or existing species can be used for comparison. However, in contexts where there are no precisely comparable or proxy goods or services on the market this methodology is inadequate. New metrics are needed as social organisations often work in these market failure spaces to meet the inadequate provision of a particular social or environmental good by creating a radically new solution to an old problem.

Despite the inherent difficulties presented, there is a wealth of different types of tools and method-ologies being used to try to measure progress at the different stages of the social innovation process. Some of these have been used for decades, such as participatory rural appraisal techniques and cost-benefit analysis and others have emerged more recently with the increased demand to assess the impact of social innovations such as social return on investment and outcome benchmarks.[60] The table below highlights examples for each stage.

Table 28. Examples of how to measure social innovation

SOCIAL INNOVATION STAGE	MEASUREMENT TOOLS
1. Prompts, inspiration, dialogue	Participatory rural appraisal · Mapping (systems, resources, assets, needs, flows) · Action research · Systems thinking models · Online petitions.
2. Proposals and ideas	Investment appraisal & cost–benefit analysis · User surveys, online voting & wikis · Forum theatre · Ideas banks & suggestion booths · Citizens' juries & panels.
3. Prototyping and pilots	Randomised control trials · Stated preference & "willingness to pay" · Beta testing & open testing · Slow & fast prototyping · User surveys.
4. Sustaining	Business model analysis based on incomes & outcomes · Social impact investment appraisal · Social venture capital appraisal · User-generated metrics & user experience · Balanced scorecard & CSR reporting.
5. Scaling and diffusion	Social accounting matrices · Compliance with labels & standards · Social targets · Franchise and licence uptake · Social impact assessment · Social return on investment · Blended value accounting · Enhanced social audit.
6. Systemic change	Outcome benchmarks · Existence of new systems (infrastructure, production systems, regulation, coalitions, movements, financial models).

Source: Murray et al. 2011

---

60 An example of an outcome benchmark is the use of local surveys to measure answers to questions such as how well people get on with each other in a neighbourhood or whether they feel a sense of influence over decisions, rather than using indicators chosen by individual organisations to prove their impact.

Blended value

An important concept to be considered in the debate on how to measure the impact of social innovation is the idea of "blended value", a theory established by Emerson and other authors in 2003 with the publication of the "Blended Value Map", which tracks the intersections and opportunities of economic, social and environmental value creation. The theory is built on the premise that organisations create financial and social value, that these are interconnected and that, in some cases, they are mutually supportive rather than opposing forces. Blended value has been applied to investment appraisal, integrating environmental and social risks and opportunities into securities valuation, real estate and other financial sectors. A spectrum of blended value accounting methodologies has been developed ranging from pure financial accounting to environmental accounting with a diversity of models in between, as highlighted in the table below.

Box 12. Blended value accounting

> *"Value is what gets created when investors invest and organisations act to pursue their mission. Traditionally, we have thought of value as being either economic (and created by for-profit companies) or social (and created by non-profit or non-governmental organisations).*
>
> *What the Blended Value Proposition states is that all organisations, whether for-profit or not, create value that consists of economic, social and environmental value components – and that investors (whether market-rate, charitable or some mix of the two) simultaneously generate all three forms of value through providing capital to organisations.*
>
> *The outcome of all this activity is value creation and that value is itself non-divisible and, therefore, a blend of these three elements."*

Source: Emerson 2003

Accounting mechanisms

Alongside the development of the many tools to assess and measure the different stages of social innovation, many reporting mechanisms have been evolved to formalise disclosure of social, environmental and financial impacts of any given social innovation. These range from financial accounts based on purely quantitative data to social audits accounting for social impact assessed with qualitative data. The figure below shows the spectrum of some of these reporting mechanisms based on the overarching theory of blended value and they are described in more detail in Table 29.

Figure 24. The spectrum of Blended Value Accounting

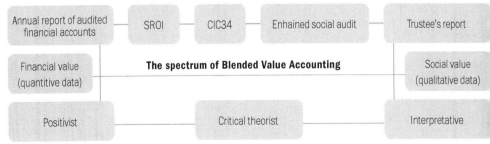

Table 29. Examples of Blended Value Accounting

Annual report of audited financial accounts

All social enterprises registered as companies or charities are obliged to produce an annual report of audited financial accounts, often included as part of a larger, more descriptive report of the organisation's activities.

Inspiring example: Café Direct Annual Reports[61]

Social Return on Investment (SROI)

The SROI report, first developed by the Roberts Enterprise Development Fund in 1999, has three parts;

1. The full blended value of a project, combining enterprise/financial value creation and a monetised representation of its social impact value
2. The financial investment in the project and
3. The blended return on investment (combining financial and social return).

Inspiring example: Wise Group SROI report[62]

Community Interest Company Report (CIC34)

As well as financial reports, Community Interest Companies are required to produce a CIC34 report of activities, stakeholder consultation, details of their directors' remuneration and other aspects of their operations.

Inspiring example: Develop your child CIC report[63]

Enhanced social audit

Provides descriptive metrics, as well as financial information, in contrast to a CSR report for a business, which reports on the complementary social or environmental activity that complements core business. This type of report focuses on progress towards an organisation's social mission.

Inspiring example: Furniture Resource Centre Group's Report
"We're Doing Good, Aren't We?"[64]

Trustees' report

Obligatory report for UK charities setting out principal aims and objectives and progress made as well as structure, governance and management arrangements, and possibly a financial overview.

Inspiring example: Hackney Community Transport Annual Report and Accounts[65]

Source: Nicholls 2009

---

61 Café Direct's annual reports from 2005 are available at www.cafédirect.co.uk.

62 Wise Group's SROI report included 12 financial indicators: welfare benefit savings from temporary employment; increased income for participants; increased employability of those not entering employment; increased future earning potential arising from qualifications achieved; and, finally, drugs and mental health outcomes. The SROI analysis suggested that, for every £1 spent, £4.65 had been realised in added value and that this equated to £14,989 per participant.

63 Reports available at www.developyourchild.co.uk.

64 Reports available at www.frcgroup.co.uk.

65 Reports available at www.hctgroup.org.

Measuring social impact at the macro level

Attempts to measure social impact and social innovation are also being developed at the macro level, and the work of Joseph Stiglitz and others undertaken through the Commission on the Measurement of Economic Performance and Social Progress[66] is a good example of this. The Commission was set up by the French President Sarkozy in 2008 to analyse the limitations of GDP as a performance and progress indicator, propose alternative indicators and assess the viability of using them to measure social well-being and quality of life. Among other indicators the Commission uses the mean income of a country as a more accurate indicator of economic well-being than that of GDP. Alternative means of reporting on social impact are also being developed in the UK to measure progress within the framework of the government's Big Society[67] initiative and in the White House's Council for Community Solutions.[68]

———

Key references

Emerson, J. (2003)
The Blended Value Proposition: Integrating Social and Financial Returns.
California Management Review, Summer 2003.

Nicholls, A. (2008)
Capturing the Performance of the Socially Entrepreneurial Organization (SEO): An Organizational Legitimacy Approach in Robinson, J., Mair, J., & Hockerts, K. (eds.), *International Perspectives on Social Entrepreneurship Research*, Palgrave MacMillan, pp. 27-74.

Nicholls, A. (2009)
We Do Good Things Don't We? Blended Value Accounting in Social Entrepreneurship. *Accounting, Organisations and Society*, 34.6–7, pp. 755-769.

Phills, Jr., J.A., Deilglmeier, K., & Miller, D.T. (2008)
Rediscovering Social Innovation, *Stanford Social Innovation Review*, Fall 2008.

Stiglitz, J., Sen, A., & Fitoussi, J.-P. (2009)
Report of the Commission on the Measurement of Economic Performance and Social Progress.

US Socially Responsible Investment Forum (2010)
Socially Responsible Investment Trends 2010. Social Investment Forum Foundation.

---

66 www.stiglitz-sen-fitoussi.fr

67 www.thebigsociety.co.uk

68 www.serve.gov/council_home.asp#maincontent

Cross-sector collaboration

There is a general consensus among leading practitioners, academics and philanthropists that social innovation cuts across the traditional boundaries of business, government and civil society. In this new hybrid economy roles are shifting and evolving and new hybrid organisational models are emerging. Following a review of this changing landscape, we highlight some of the conditions for successful social innovation in this context of cross-sector collaboration.

Social innovation was traditionally filled on one side by civil society (from an individual household level to grant giving foundations and campaigning institutions), and, on the other, by governments who pioneered social innovation through public sector reforms and the creation of the welfare state in the 19th century. In other words markets' failure to provide adequate social and environmental welfare was addressed by key sectors generally in isolation of each other. Today these silos have largely disappeared and social innovations are now being initiated by individual social entrepreneurs, business intrapreneurs, government departments, academic centres and international networks. In 2004, authors writing for the recently launched *Stanford Social Innovation Review* described on the one hand an explosion of business practices applied to non-profit organisations and governments and on the other more businesses adopting social programmes. The dissolution of the boundaries between public, private and non-profit sectors was also discussed (Dees *et al.* 2004).

> This shift in roles shows governments taking a less regulatory role and working in partnership with the private and non-profit sectors, businesses taking on social causes and non-profit organisations learning from the commercial sector. In addition the free flow of ideas, values, relationships and finance across these sectors helps to fuel contemporary social innovation, which is prompting recognition of the value of relational capital. Organisations across all these sectors dedicate considerable resources to engaging with their key stakeholders to build relational capital through open events, participation in networks and associations, active social networks and websites for example (Phills 2008).

The social economy and key interfaces

The dichotomy between the social economy and the market economy is now shifting, as is the relationship between private and public goods with production for the masses changing to production by the masses. Take for example the 18 million cancer-related websites that have been created largely by individuals and families affected by the disease. Murray *et al.* have identified four key actors in the social economy, and these are illustrated below.

Figure 25. The social economy

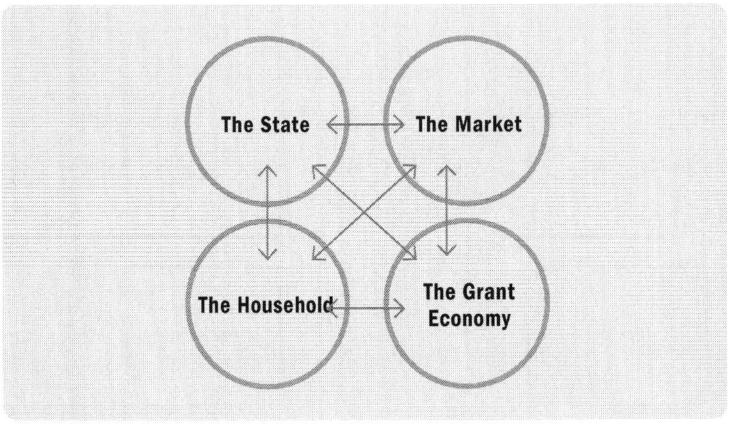

Source: The Young Foundation

Within the framework that structures the interaction of the four key economic actors, Murray *et al.* describe social innovation as the creation of a series of social outputs and outcomes which derive not from any one subset of the economy, but rather are generated at the interfaces between the actors' particular sectors, as indicated by the shaded area. None of the economies is exclusively concerned with social innovation. The market, for example, although largely private, is increasingly engaged with the social economy through CSR programmes or specific concerns such as fair trade and environmental goods; the household also has certain private ambitions, but participates in the social economy through informal networks, associations and social movements. The binary positions between market and state need to be contextualised into a more complex set of relationships as the market is embedded in the state, and vice versa, and they thus both develop new relationships with civil society and the grant economy.

The recognition that social innovation stems from multiple sources has led leading thinkers on social innovation to identify firstly, a series of emerging trends such as the growth of mutual action among individuals in the household economy (open-source software, web-based social networking, peer-to-peer collaboration, etc.); and, secondly, and very notably, the growth of social enterprises within the market economy, such as companies with a social mission like the Mondragon[69] cooperative, which has operations worldwide in banking, manufacturing and higher education, BRAC,[70] the developing world's largest NGO, or the Grameen Bank.[71] The role of the grant economy and the state in supporting peer-to-peer collaboration and the role of the household and the state in social enterprises is complex and evolving; the figure below highlights some of the elements to consider at

---

69 Mondragon is a cooperative business that was founded in the Basque country in 1956 and now provides 85,000 jobs across the world in finance, industry, distribution and education: www.mondragon-corporation.com.

70 BRAC is a development organisation dedicated to alleviating poverty by empowering the poor to bring about change in their own lives, offering microfinancing among other services: www.brac.net.

71 Grameen Bank was one of the founding institutions to deliver microcredits to the poor and currently has 8,349 million borrowers: www.grameen-info.org.

each interface between the four actors' particular sub-sectors of involvement in the social economy. The diagram below shows the forms of interaction typical at each interface. For example, between the state and the market economy there are fiscal and regulatory interactions, whereas between the household and the grant economy volunteering and participation in social movements are common interactions.

Figure 26. Interfaces across the social economy

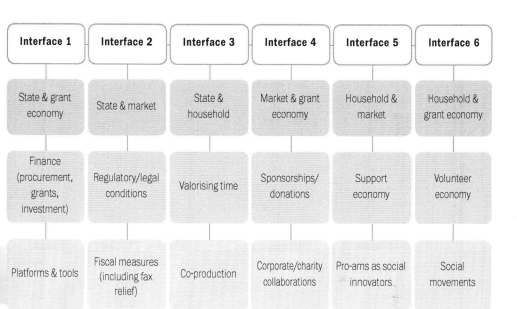

The relationships between universities, industry and government are another set of cross-sector collaboration that has attracted attention as universities are playing an increasingly important role in innovation in knowledge-based societies. There has been a shift from the situation in which the state controls academia and industry to more dynamic systems in which each plays a more active role in a trilateral network of hybrid organisations (Etzkowitz & Loet Leydesdorff 2000).

Hybrid organisational models

Within the evolving hybrid economy of shifting roles and new interactions between the sub-sectors of the social economy, a set of hybrid organisational models has also been observed which often fulfil the multifaceted roles of generating blended value. Most countries have their own specific legislation regarding these hybrid organisations and the table below highlights some of the better-known examples:

Table 30. Different types of social organisation

COUNTRY	LEGAL FORM	DETAILS
UK	Community Interest Company (CIC)	Established in 2005 to give a unique identity to companies with a social mission, so that they could be more easily identified and recognised by the grant-making economy and investors. To date, over 2,500 CICs have been established.
Spain, Italy	Social cooperative	Company owned and managed by the people who use its services (a consumer cooperative) and/or by the people who work there (worker cooperative).
US	501 (c)	In the US, there are 28 types of non-profit organisation including the 501(c), which is exempt from taxes in certain states.
India	Section 25 Company	A company set up to promote commerce, art, science, religion, charity or any other useful activity provided the profits or other income is only used to promote the company and no dividend is paid to its members.
Ukraine	Sole Proprietorship Company	Appoints a board member as the owner rather than the original entrepreneur to protect against mission drift.

Source: Phills 2008

Each type of organisation has its own particular reporting mechanisms, some regulated and others voluntary, and, in addition to these legally determined structures, there are a number of other more informal models such as social business partnerships, CSR hybrid models, such as Vodafone's MPESA[72] programme, corporate non-profit management of social provision, partnerships and business engagement models.

Collective impact

Another type of organisational model used to bring about social change is that referred to as collective impact. Collective impact has been used to describe "the commitment of a group of important actors from different sectors to a common agenda for solving a specific social problem" (Kanier & Kramer 2011). Two clear examples of collective impact are the UK government's Big Society, a government-led initiative engaging the household economy, civil society and business in pursuit of a set of common goals cutting across diverse social issues such as health, education, crime and the environment. The aim is to empower civil society to engage in public sector reform (NEF 2011) by giving families, neighbourhoods, cooperatives, social enterprises and small businesses the responsibility to take more action towards addressing social and environmental imbalances at a local level. The White House Council for Community Solutions uses a similar bottom-up approach to engage civil society in key social challenges. Both initiatives have received criticism as merely ways of increasing voluntary action to reduce public spending without paying attention to the systemic changes needed to address existing inequalities. Evidence of the effectiveness of this

---

72 MPESA is the product name of a mobile-phone-based money transfer service for Safaricom, which is a Telkom Kenya and Vodafone affiliate: www.safaricom.co.ke.

approach is still limited; however, these examples illustrate the potential for greater progress towards large-scale social change. But for it to really be effective the approach needs a far broader movement of individuals and organisations from non-profit organisations, governments, businesses and the public working together towards a common goal (NEF 2010).

Isolated impact

At the opposite end of the collaboration spectrum is what has been described as isolated impact, *"an approach oriented toward finding and funding a solution embodied within a single organisation, combined with the hope that the most effective organisations will grow or replicate to extend their impact more widely"* (Kanier & Kramer 2011). Many social sector organisations continue with isolated impact such as public–private partnerships, or interactions between the grant economy and non-profits to address a specific social problem without the involvement of the market or the state. This is evident when non-profit organisations competing for a particular grant tend to demonstrate their potential as individual organisations competent to meet the given challenge rather than their relational capital – thereby revealing the isolated impact trap. While no single organisation can be blamed for creating the world's problems, it is evident that no single organisation is able to fix them. Advocates of collective impact suggest that the shift from isolated to collective impact requires a systemic approach that focuses on the relationships between organisations and progress towards shared objectives (Kanier & Kramer 2011).

Cross-fertilisation, bees, trees and pollinators

How to foster effective cross-sector collaboration is another area of debate that has been running since John Elkington's ground-breaking publication *Cannibals with Forks* in 1997, in which he discussed the symbiosis of partnerships between government, civil society and industry and the idea of co-opetition (a neologism coined to describe cooperative competition) was established. This has more recently developed into the concept of cross-fertilisation, and the notion of influencing from the edge to refer to social innovations initial penetration of the business sector. The work of the Biomimicry Institute[73] is a clear example of this. It is a non-profit foundation set up by leading biologists and environmentalists to study the potential offered by natural patterns, processes and systems as models to be replicated in product and service design. A group of open-minded business leaders have taken on board their ideas and integrated them into innovation processes and this has had outstanding results in a range of sectors from architecture to sanitation.

Another example of cross-fertilisation is that of the General Electric Company which developed its "ecoimagination challenge"[74] inspired, and perhaps pressured, by the environmental sector. The initiative made $70 billion in the first five years. The retail supply chain Marks & Spencer's[75] initiative "Look behind the label", which was influenced by the fair trade movement and animal rights and other pressure groups, has also been remarkably successful to the extent that other companies are following suit. *"I think we are in one of those periods where for several reasons you are going to see creative destruction on a scale that is almost unparalleled. The question then is where in the world do you look for clues as to what the new business models, the new mind-sets, the new technologies might look like and how they might operate. The answer*

---

[73] http://biomimicry.net

[74] www.ecomagination.com

[75] www.marksandspencer.com

is very rarely that you would look at the incumbent companies because they are still operating and trying to do it more efficiently with the old models and the old mind-sets. Where you tend to look is on the edges of the systems and that's where you'd expect the new solutions to come from" (John Elkington interviewed by INSEAD in 2011).

As previously discussed, the free flow of information and financial resources across sectors and boundaries assists the cross-fertilisation of ideas; however, effective collaboration and the potential for scale is more likely when there is an interaction between the bees (small agile organisations or entrepreneurs who are able to cross-pollinate their ideas) and the trees (larger institutions with roots and resilience). The role of connectors, brokers and entrepreneurs, who link ideas, resources and financing, is also especially valuable and the growing sector of international networks such as the Social Innovation Exchange[76] is beginning to create this network of networks to further stimulate social innovation.

Conditions for success

Kanier and Kramer have proposed five key conditions for successful, collective impact initiatives which can be used as guidelines for maximising the social impact of any cross-sector collaboration; they are as follows:

Common agenda: a shared vision for change, including a common understanding of the problem and a joint approach to solving it through agreed actions in order to avoid energies and resources being diverted in different directions. Considerable effort may be needed to achieve this and funders can play a key role here.

Shared measurement: a common set of indicators helps to ensure all parties are aligned as well as being held accountable and able to learn from each other's successes and failures.

Mutually reinforcing activities: not just strength in numbers as the power of collective action results from coordinated activities with clear divisions of responsibilities to address the multiple causes of social problems.

Continuous communication: developing trust across non-profit organisations, businesses, governments and civil society organisations is crucial for the effectiveness of any collaboration, and this is enhanced by well-organised regular meetings and clear communication channels.

Backbone support: dedicated staff to plan, manage and support the initiative, as well as provide communication, administration and technological resources to ensure the initiative is run smoothly.

---

76 www.socialinnovationexchange

———

Key references

Bastianel, T. (2011)
Big Society or Collective Impact? *Stanford Social Innovation Review*.

Dees, G., Battle Anderson, B., & Wei-skillern, J. (2004)
Scaling Social Impact: Strategies for spreading social innovations. *Stanford Social Innovation Review*.

Elkington, J. (2008)
Cannibals with Forks: The Triple Bottom Line of 21st Century Business.
Capstone Publishers.

Etzkowitz, H., & Leydesdorff, L. (2000)
The Dynamics of Innovation from National Systems and Mode 2 to a Triple Helix of University–Industry–Government Relations. *Research Policy* 29 (109-123)

Kania, J., & Kramer, M. (2011)
Collective Impact. *Stanford Social Innovation Review*, No. 43, Winter.

Murray, R., Caulier-Grice, J., & Mulgan, G. (2010)
The Open Book of Innovation. The Young Foundation and NESTA.

NEF (2010)
Cutting It: The Big Society and the New Austerity. New Economics Foundation.

Phills, Jr., J.A., Deilglmeier, K., & Miller, D.T. (2008)
Rediscovering Social Innovation, *Stanford Social Innovation Review*, Fall 2008.

Economic sustainability and long-term viability

What makes social enterprises different from traditional socially oriented organisations is their ability to generate financial value as well as social value, and in principle they use this blended value to sustain themselves in the future. While the field of social innovation is increasingly populated with financial support mechanisms to help kick-start initiatives, less attention has been paid to achieving long-term viability. Therefore, we now turn to explore the complex relationship between social innovation and economic sustainability.

A commonly recognised challenge for any socially oriented organisation is acquiring capital; this is an essential component in building an organisation, whether profit or non-profit, in order to bring services to clients and customers, to grow, prosper and sustain itself into the future. In addition, the social capital market, like any other, requires efficiency, transparency and measurable outcomes for sustained growth; however, these characteristics are not always achieved, resulting in a situation that has been described as the "Capital Challenge" (Emerson 2006).

Capital challenge

Key concerns expressed about the social capital market are 1) high transaction costs, 2) an inadequate information flow, 3) a lack of market responsiveness, 4) limited connections between organisational performance and capital allocation, 5) a shortage of common standards and definitions, 6) a need for more intermediation and, finally, 7) a dearth of common understanding of the relationships between risk and various returns. In addition to these Emerson claims that the available financial instruments (largely grants and loans) are not adequate for creating real capital investment in emerging for-profit social ventures that are trying to scale up their activity (Emerson 2006).

In this context, one of the key challenges for social enterprises is sustaining growth over time. This is partly due to the limited access to risk and growth capital, as well as specialist technical knowledge about risk and growth, but it also results from the difficulty of balancing conflicting economic, social and environmental pressures. While much has been written on the triple bottom line, social returns on investment and blended value, the question of how to ensure the social mission remains a critical question for social enterprises and continues to dominate investors' concerns (Elkington 2008).

In his article on what he called "Capitalism 3.0", Emerson recommended a series of building blocks to address this challenge and enhance the conditions for sustained growth. He defined this approach as "an opportunity to step out of the limits we've created ourselves and a common way to understand the nature of value and organise to maximum value". These building blocks are described below:

Box 13. Strategies for Capitalism 3.0

- Map the social capital market through types of returns, terms of investment and risk
- Define the market for a new asset class focused on blended returns (exploring investor motivation and risk profiles)
- Develop policy frameworks that are supportive of practitioners' and investors' needs (at international and national levels)
- Encourage viable strategies for capital diversification (investors can already receive full market return on securities offered by certain non-profit organisations such as Habitat for Humanity)
- Expand the role of funding intermediaries
- Call on foundations to take the lead in creating investment instruments structured to generate multiple returns for both investors and practitioners
- Develop new forms of collaboration capable of creating greater efficiencies, mobilising investment capital and sharing emerging practices
- Diversify corporate capital
- Create an international fund to provide secondary financing

Source: Emerson & Bonini 2006

Financial support mechanisms

While long-term growth remains a key challenge, there is a host of financial mechanisms to support social innovation in its early stages of development. These range from grants offered by foundations and philanthropic individuals, investment funds from the SRI sector, a range of public finance mechanisms and online platforms for individual donations. Here, we highlight just a few of the mechanisms available in each sector.

From the grant economy: this may seem the most obvious port of call for a new social innovation and opportunities range from direct funding for individual social entrepreneurs, such as that offered by Ashoka, the Skoll Foundation and UnLtd, to awards and recognition prizes. There are now 25 philanthropic organisations across the world which give social-innovation-related awards and prizes often for sums of around $50,000, such as for example the Schwab Foundation awards. Other grant mechanisms include fast grants, term-limited charities where funding is given for a limited period of time, competitions and challenges such as the XFoundation's $10m prize for challenges related to sustainable cars or the human genome. Micro-grants to fund small R&D activities are also common, as are donations and social investment for social enterprises.

The role of intermediaries in the grant-giving economy is increasingly significant, helping to connect donors to projects, particularly on a micro scale such as the giving platform Kiva, philanthropic "e-bays" and other donor platforms. Mission-related investment is also a growing sector stimulating social innovation through various mechanisms such as strategic investment from the Bill Gates Foundation, venture philanthropy from the Robert Wood Johnson Foundation and philanthropic mutual funds such as the Acumen Fund, to name a few significant examples. Issues of governance and accountability, training and capacity, as well as regulation and reporting are common concerns across the grant-giving economy for social innovation.

From the market economy: the second door to knock on for financing social innovation is the private sector's. Individual businesses' Corporate Social Responsibility programmes often include a mix of grant-giving to social initiatives such as Unilever's support of the Marine Stewardship Council; hybrid business models, such as Vodafone's MPESA; and strategic partnerships, such as those of Grameen-Danone or BASF-Gain. Company commitments to support a certain social sector is another source of finance for social innovation: for example, Walmart's pledge for renewable energy or certi-fied organic produce.

Ethical investing, as already mentioned, is a huge growth sector,[77] which takes in a wide range of things from public pension funds adopting ethical guidelines, as is the case for the Norwegian Government Pension Fund, to mission-connected social impact investment from foundations with key interests in particular issues such as fair trade or environmental technology. Social enterprise funds and new venture capital is another emerging sector, with Triodos Bank serving as a clear example of a financial institution that solely invests in enterprises demonstrating social or environmental value generation. Social venture funds such as Bridges or Community Venture in the UK are another mechanism for start-ups. In addition to these there are charitable loans, such as those offered by the Charity Bank in the UK, and charitable equity funds, which allow charities to invest in start-ups, provide philanthropic investment for growth and R&D mentoring funds. A good example of the last of these is the international cooperative Mondragon's financial affiliate Caja Laboral, which provides start-up lending credit to new cooperatives.

The launch of social finance institutions is a growing sector. These range from ethical banks such as Triodos, the UK Cooperative Bank and Banca Etica in Italy to the Spanish and Italian Coopera-tive Banks, which are owned by their members and governed according to a one-member one-vote system. Another source of social finance are Credit Unions, which are slightly different from coopera-tives in that they do not lend externally. These are particularly strong in Canada, where the national federation of Credit Unions has 427 members. There are also other financing structures to be consid-ered such as financial guarantee cooperatives, socially motivated intermediaries like Zopa, business angels and social wholesale banks.

On the less institutional level, peer-to-peer lending, pioneered by Kiva, is becoming an increasingly main-stream option for financing social initiatives, as is both the microcredits sector, in which Grameen Bank, BRAC and ASA are key players, and the new area of financing, crowdfunding. Alternative currencies such

---

77 According to the Social Investment Forum, social investment in the US now accounts for 11% of total assets under management. A recent Young Foundation study found that a total of £165m in social investments were made in the UK last year.

as the Totnes Pound are also being established in various European countries and Japan as a mechanism to support local economies that focuses on local production and consumption.

From the public sector: governments are key players at the interfaces of social innovation being prompted by a political interest in providing social goods, as well as an increasing need to interact with the market economy and civil society to achieve these targets. Internal financing mechanisms include "top-slicing" departmental budgets for innovation, dedicated innovation funds such as the $700m US education innovation fund or the UK's NHS £220m innovation fund, cross-cutting budgets, holistic local budgets and outcome-based budgets. Other innovative public finance tools include online budget setting systems like the Australian budget calculator, social clauses in public contracts and innovation-related pay.

Public innovation funds also have a strong role in supporting innovation: for example, India's National Innovation Foundation, which supports grassroots innovation, or Finland's Innovation Fund, which conducts research and development. Other funds act as internal public venture funds such as the UK's Invest to Save budget for cross-cutting innovation, or Singapore's Enterprise Challenge. Some governments are also branching into service innovation, as is the case with both India's and the UK's Regional Innovation Funds.

Citizen engagement in financing social innovation is another area that is becoming more popular, with examples such as participatory budgeting in which citizens define local priorities, and also public voting on grant allocation, as undertaken in the Big Lottery Fund Competition "the people's 50 million". Tracking public finance and open-source auditing are additional mechanisms for involving citizens in public investing.

Taxes levied to induce socially responsible behaviour can offer a valuable stimulus for social innovation: exemptions from traffic congestion charges for electric vehicles encourage green transport alternatives , and landfill tax offers a source of motivation for recycling initiatives. Other examples include urban improvement levies, such as the Olympic levy in London, or voluntary city taxes as introduced by Antanus Mockus in Bogotá. Another common fiscal mechanism to support social innovation is the role of tax exemption for charities and non-profit organisations.

Finally, governments also play a role as investors through local bonds, social investment funds, such as the UK Department of Health's £100m social enterprise investment fund, social enterprise investment funds, hybrid financing, joint ventures, public finance initiatives and preventative investment such as the US Justice Reinvestment Programme.

Social investment frameworks

Given the wealth of different types of social innovation, as well as the diverse financial requirements at each stage of the initiative's development, it is not surprising that such a myriad of investment opportunities has arisen. Recognised authors have developed a series of frameworks to help organise this diverse spectrum according to the different levels of involvement demanded by investors, the different stages of a social enterprise's development and its level of maturity. One example of this, illustrated in Figure 27, is Bolton's Two Axis Investment Vehicle map showing the various degrees of involvement of different types of investor, ranging from the charitable to the commercial.

Figure 27. Bolton's Two Axis Investment Vehicle Map

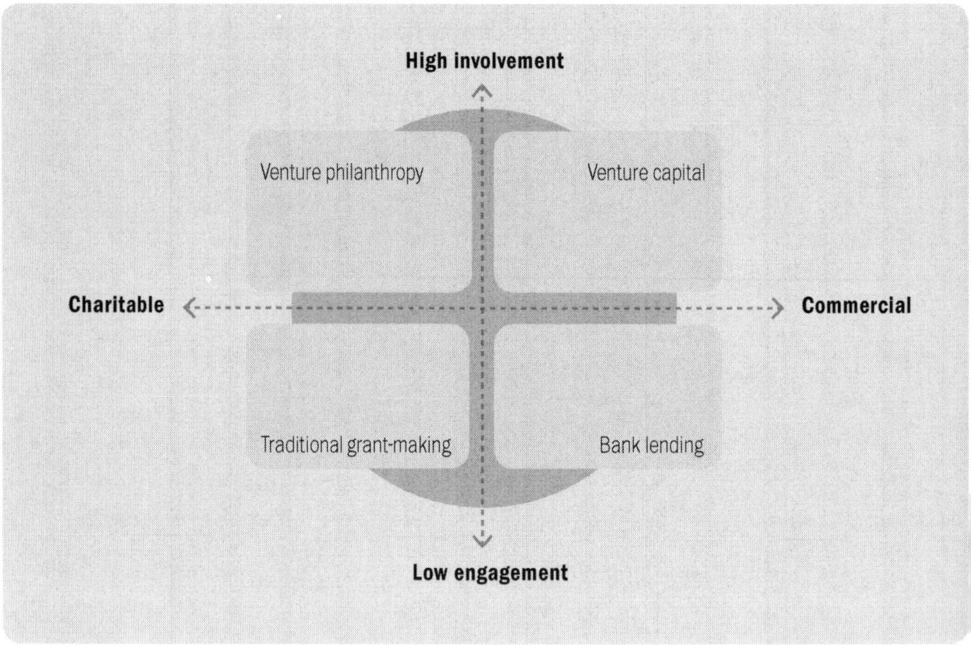

Source: Emerson & Spitzer 2007

A second example is offered by Emerson's Capital Framework, which provides a more complex map of different types of investors and considers three variables: the development stage of the organisation, from start-up to exit stage; the age of the initiative; and its strategic orientation, whether maximising economic value, social value or working within the hybrid enterprise space. Figure 28 illustrates where different investors are located within this framework.

Figure 28. Emerson's Capital Framework, Adapted from Gregory Dees

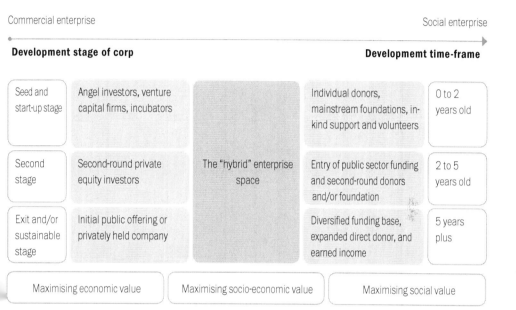

Source: Emerson & Spitzer 2007

Non-profit funding models

A key challenge for many players in the social innovation field is the lack of connection between beneficiaries and clients. Typically a non-profit organisation will channel finance from those who can pay (clients) to those who can't (beneficiaries), which therefore requires two business models, one for the programme and one for its financing. Non-profit organisations typically have a high level of sophistication in delivering programmes to the beneficiaries, but operate with far less clarity when it comes to financing. In a survey of US non-profit organisations it was shown that 45% of mid-size organisations have less than three months of operating reserves and 1 in 4 mid-size organisations say their top financial objective is to break even (rather than generate cash reserves or a surplus for down years).[78] The for-profit sector, where the client is the beneficiary of the service or product, has of course much greater financial clarity. Authors Foster, Kim and Christensen have developed a useful categorisation of different types of non-profit funding models that helps provide clarity around which model is most appropriate, as shown in Table 31.

78 http://socialinnovation.ca/community/buzz/scary-numbers-brave-members-most-nonprofits-small-businesses-are-suffering-from-finan

Table 31. 10 Non-profit funding models

MODEL	FUNDING	STRATEGY
Heartfelt connector	Many individual donations	Causes that resonate with a wide public at all income levels. Simple, concise messages, identify issues that resonate.
Beneficiary builder	Many individual donations	Rely on people they have given service to (e.g. hospitals, universities), and ongoing relationships with beneficiaries. Address issues that provide individual service as well as social good.
Member motivator	Many individual donations	Offer services identified as sought after by members. Address issues integral to members' everyday lives and uses fundraising activities that involve members.
Big better	Single person, few individuals/ foundations	Tackle a specific issue of personal interest to key funders, often environmental (a particular piece of land) or medical. Identify wealthy individuals interested in the cause and go for major long-lasting impact.
Public provider	Government funding	Work in partnership with public agencies to deliver key social services (e.g. social services, housing and education). It is important for an organisation to demonstrate a better service delivery than competitors.
Policy innovator	Government funding	Model solutions to provide social goods that are more effective and less expensive. Offer innovative approaches for lasting change, requiring government partnership.
Beneficiary broker	Government funding	Organisations that compete for public funding to deliver a key social service, needing to demonstrate superiority of service
Resource recycler	Corporate funding	Take in-kind contributions from individuals and organisations and redistribute them to those in need. Need to attract additional funding to cover overheads.
Market maker	Mix of funders	Mix of altruistic donors and payment from market forces, particularly when for ethical reasons operating under normal market conditions is not appropriate (e.g. paying for liver transplants). Group of funders with financial interests, often health-related.
Local nationaliser	Mix of funders	National network of local organisations with local funding on issues of local relevance (housing, education, etc.). Supported by individual and corporate donations with very little government funding.

Sustainable value creation

To conclude this section we would like to underscore the need for more research on successful business models for social innovation. While, as noted, there are great opportunities to initiate social innovation, there is limited understanding of successful sustainable value creation. Lessons can be taken from the world of CSR where performance-driven, collaborative, innovative and accountable initiatives with a clear purpose are those that survive. Tania Ellis, a leading Danish author on socially responsible business opportunities, sets out 4 Cs as key components in sustainable value creation: Clear purpose (including commitment from the CEO), Corporate engagement (where CSR is hard- and soft-wired across the organisation), Collaborative co-creation (where key stakeholders become key partners) and Clear communication (with a focus on openness and transparency).

———

Key references

Bugg-Levine, B., & Emerson, J. (2011)
Impact Investing. Transforming how we make money while we make a difference.
Jossey Bass.

Ellis, T. (2012)
The New Pioneers. Sustainable Business Success through Social Innovation and Social Entrepreneurship.
John Wiley & Sons.

Emerson, J., & Spitzer, J. (2007)
From Fragmentation to Function: Critical Concepts and Writings on Social Capital Markets' Structure, Operation, and Innovation.
Skoll Centre for Social Entrepreneurship, Oxford Saïd Business School.

Emerson, J., & Bonini, S. (2006)
Capitalism 3.0. Exploring the Future of Capital Investing and Value Creation.
www.blendedvalue.org.

Foster, W., Kim, P., & Christiansen, B. (2009)
10 Non Profit Funding Models. *Stanford Social Innovation Review*, 26, Spring 2009.

Murray, R., Caulier-Grice, J., & Mulgan, G. (2010)
The Open Book of Innovation. The Young Foundation and NESTA.

Nicholls, A. (2009)
We Do Good Things, Don't We? Blended Value Accounting In Social Entrepreneurship. *Accounting, Organisations and Society*, 34.6–7, pp. 755-769

Innovation type

Although social innovation builds on a great deal of robust research around innovation in the fields of medicine, technology and business, it is still an immature science. There is little consensus on the models that are most suited for addressing social problems. The following pages explore some of the different types of social innovation, with a particular focus on open innovation as a dynamic mechanism for accelerating social change, as well as the key challenges faced by social innovators.

The Austrian economist and political scientist Schumpeter was one of the first to define different types of innovation, often referred to as Mark 1 and Mark 2, the first being instigated by entrepreneurs or "wild spirits" and the second model driven by large companies with the resources and capital to invest in research and development. As has been outlined in previous chapters, social innovation in fact stems from a broader spectrum of actors – governments, social enterprises, grant-giving bodies and individual households – and it arises across a complex interface of connections between these different economic subsets. According to Schumpeter's formulation of the process of creative destruction, innovation has the power to destroy the old to open the way for the new, and this appears to remain true today. Contemporary social innovations can generally be seen to follow the same process as the new "truths" of the early 20th century, at first ridiculed, then violently opposed before finally being accepted as self-evident. Take, for example, the "tree huggers" such as Swampy who was the media focus of the Newbury A34 road protest in the UK and the other protestors, who were ridiculed by the press as late as the 1990s, who are now today's leading sustainability consultants.

Product or process

There are two streams of research on innovation: firstly that which explores innovation as a process that is dependent on individual creativity, organisational structure, environmental context and social or economic factors. The other focuses on the outcome in the form of new products, increasingly services, and also production methods (Nicholls 2008). Policy-makers, practitioners and funders are often seeking mechanisms to design contexts that support innovation (take MyBnk's[79] recent "hackathon" where a group of hackers were put in a warehouse for 48 hours to design mobile applications around financial literacy), or Google's office environment where relaxation and play are important elements that have been integrated into the design.

Outcome-based innovation sparks an ongoing interest in which a new idea will prosper. Whether outcome- or output-based, innovation by definition needs to be not only new or novel, but better or more effective than its predecessor. According to the innovation guru Clayton Christensen, for something to be a social innovation, social change should be its "primary objective" and not just a "largely unintended by-product" Other authors claim a social innovation should also be more effective, just and sustainable, as well as generating more social value than individual value regardless of the original motivations (Phills 2008).

---

79 MyBnk is an NGO targeted at improving the financial literacy of young people through innovative learning experiences: www.mybnk.org.

Radical or incremental

Christensen has developed this discussion by distinguishing catalytic (social) innovation from disruptive (commercial) innovations. The latter he describes as *"a process by which a product or service takes root initially in simple applications at the bottom of a market and then relentlessly moves 'up market', eventually displacing established competitors"* (Christensen 2006). This debate is situated within the context of the long-standing discussion around incremental and radical innovation that began in the 1970s. This dichotomy may be considered in terms of the internal and external dimensions of innovation. The internal dimension is based on knowledge and resources within an organisation; in this case, incremental innovation builds on existing competencies within an organisation, whereas radical innovation brings in new ideas, destroying existing competencies. In contrast, the external dimension differentiates between innovation based on technology and its impact on market competitiveness. An incremental innovation will involve improvements to existing technologies, while a radical innovation will create something entirely new, rendering predecessors obsolete.

Social entrepreneurship or intrapreneurship

Another distinction made is regarding where social innovation occurs, whether on the outside or the inside of an existing organisation and this has implications for both financing and management. Under the right conditions, according to Ellis (2012), when the 4 Cs (clear purpose, corporate engagement, collaborative co-creation and clear communication) are in place, social intrapreneurship may have the benefit of an organisation's infrastructure, financial support, human resources and research capacity, whereas, in principle, social entrepreneurs start out alone. In reality neither type of innovation is developed in isolation and both will depend on a multiple network of actors, both internal and external to the organisation. Examples of social intrapreneurship include Sam McCracken at Nike's new company Native American Business, which uses the leverage of the Nike brand to foster athletic participation among Native American communities. At CEMEX,[30] Luis Sota works with company executives to develop low-income housing solutions for Mexican consumers and, at Unilever, Vijay Sharma heads up the Shakti[81] programme, cultivating women entrepreneurs and local production in rural villages in India. The advantages and disadvantages of entre- versus intrapreneurship for social innovation are not yet clear. Whereas intrapreneurship benefits from the existing support structure, entrepreneurship, having no existing product line to protect, potentially has greater freedom to be radical.

Architectural innovation

In *Architectural Innovation,* published in 1990, Henderson and Clark argued that the radical incremental model was not enough to gauge whether one organisation was in a better position than another to engage in innovation. They identified two further dimensions, knowledge of the components and knowledge of the linkages between them (architectural knowledge), which led them to formulate the following framework. When an innovation requires both new component knowledge and new architectural knowledge it leads to radical innovation (Henderson 1990).

---

30 CEMEX has developed a low-cost house-building programme to provide quality cement housing to low-income families in Mexico: www.cemex.com.

81 Unilever's Shakti Entrepreneurial Programme helps women in rural India set up small businesses as direct-to-consumer retailers: www.unilever.com.

Figure 29. Architectural innovation

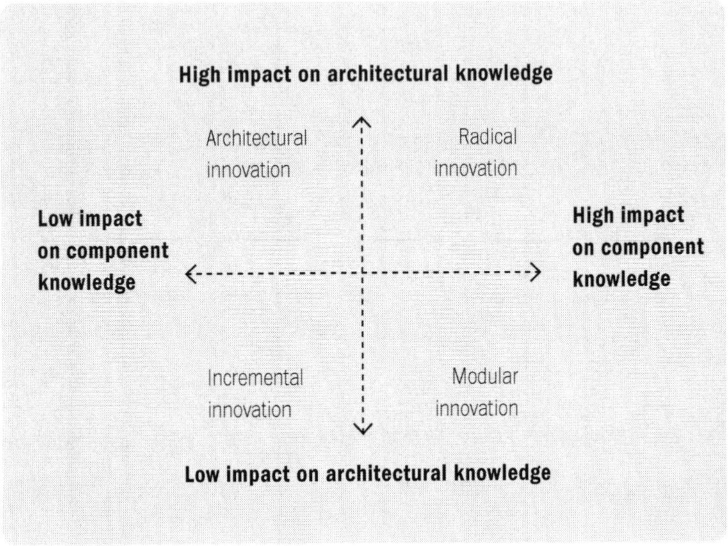

Source: Henderson 1990

This model is highly relevant to social innovation as by nature it addresses complex social prob-lems, which are multifaceted, and so require a broad architectural knowledge. According to this model the more knowledge acquired about the linkages between the multiple dimensions to the problem (whether environmental, social and economic), the more likely it is for a radical solution to be designed.

Open innovation

Open innovation is a concept that has been developed by innovation practi-tioners in the high-tech industry and has now stimulated growing interest in academia. It has been described as the *"use of purposive inflows and outflows of knowledge to accelerate internal innovation, and expand the markets for the external use of innovation"* (Chesborough *et al.* 2006). Open innovation involves the free flow of ideas, concepts and processes across stakeholder groups, the engagement of users in the design of the products and a host of tools to en-courage a diversity of inputs. This process has been shown to foster a rapid uptake of ideas, which is why it is so relevant for social innovation, where the interest is less around capitalising intellectual property and more about stimu-lating a wider uptake of an idea. The following table outlines nine principles of open innovation.

Table 32. Nine principles of open innovation

Spatial perspective	Research, technology and product development are global.
Structural perspective	Work division has increased and value chains are disaggregated.
Users' perspective	Users are integrated into the innovation process to help identify their needs.
Suppliers' perspective	Downstream side is less researched, but can provide benefits to the innovation process.
Leverage perspective	Most research is on existing markets, but this is a new area for future development.
Process perspective	Outside-in, inside-out and coupled innovation processes are possible.
Tool perspective	Instruments and tools are used so users can create their own product (e.g. SIM City).
Institutional perspective	Instead of single private investors, open to diversity of actors.
Cultural perspective	Creating a culture that values outside competence is of key importance.

Source: Chesborough et al. 2006

Methods and tools for innovation

We have already discussed some of the financial mechanisms that support social innovation, as well as the key actors involved in the process. Now we turn to some of the many methods used to stimulate the conditions for social innovation: the structure, mechanisms, systems and flows of the social economy that strengthen its capacity to develop and diffuse innovation.

In the public sector there are different organisational forms to stimulate social innovation; some of these are internal such as: individual entrepreneurs or champions, specialist innovation units, in-house innovation teams and spin-off teams (e.g. Mindlab in Denmark), quality circles to drive continuous improvement, innovation agencies, such as the UK's NHS Institute for Innovation and Improvement, and there is also public venturing. Others take the form of brokers or intermediaries, such as: the Social Innovation Exchange or Innovation Exchange in Australia, mobile innovation units, innovation accelerators, like NESTA's public service innovation laboratory, inside/outside grant administration and commissioning bodies and bridging foundations, as well as sector-specialist institutions. Finally, there are professional collaborative ventures such as communities of practice or professional learning groups.

Challenges, uncertainty and the way ahead

A key challenge for implementing and sustaining social innovation is management. Given that collaborations stretch beyond organisational boundaries, as participants in the process often only work part-time in temporary organisations, or in many cases represent various organisations at the same time, managers' habitual forms of authority and control are complicated. The extreme conditions for managers of innovation collaborations occur when uncertainties explode on the technical innovation side and there are cross-collaboration strains (Moensted 2011). A need has been identified for further reflection on how to create better management and engagement processes in distributed systems, where multiple parties collaborate in achieving a social purpose. As regards future trends, Chesborough and other authors have identified a number of areas to watch out for in open innovation and we summarise these below with reflections on how they might affect social innovation:

Box 14. Future trends in open innovation

Industry penetration
From pioneers to mainstream; software companies are opening up R&D centres on university campuses and the biomedical, technological, high-tech and software sectors are engaging in open processes.

R&D intensity
From high-tech to low-tech, open innovation is spreading to machinery, tools, medical supplies, food, consumer goods and logistics.

Large firms to SMEs
A new breed of born globals, start-ups that begin with international activity inspired by an increasing focus in business schools on open innovation.

From stand-alone to alliances
Working in collaboration: for example, Apple hired a team of 35 professionals from different companies to create the iPod.

Universities
From ivory towers to knowledge brokers with an increasing role in shaping new knowledge in collaboration with government and industry using increasing socially oriented funding mechanisms from the EU and other regions.

Processes
From amateurs to professionals with more focus on measurement; although open innovation metrics still needs more research.

Content
From product to service, which has radical implications for dematerialisation and opportunities for eco-innovation in the social economy.

Intellectual property
Shift from IP to tradable goods, which can facilitate a more rapid take-up of new ideas that work.

Source: Enkel et al. 2009

———

Key references

Storey, J. (2000)
The Management of Innovation Problem.
International Journal of Management 4(3): World Scientific Publishing Company, pages: 347-369.

Christensen, C. (1997)
The Innovator's Dilemma. When Great Technologies Cause Business to Fail.
Harvard Business School Press.

Enkel, E., Gassman, O., & Chesborough, H. (2009)
Open R&D and Open innovation: Exploring the Phenomenon.
R&D Management, 39(4), pp. 311-316.

Murray, R., Mulgan, G., & Cualier-Grice, J. (2008)
How to Innovate: The Tools for Social Innovation.
The Young Foundation.

Henderson, R., & Clarke, K. (1990)
Architectural Innovation: The Reconfiguration of Existing Product Technologies and the Failure of Established Firms. Harvard University.

Moensted, M. (2006)
Networking for Innovation. Management through Networks.
In Bernasconi, M., Harris, S., & Moensted, M. (eds.) *High-tech Entrepreneurship: Managing Innovation, Variety and Uncertainty.* Routledge, pages 242-261.

Moensted, M., & Bou, E. (2011)
Dilemmas and Challenges in Managing Innovation Collaborations: Stretching Management.
Article submitted to Technovation.

Scalability and replicability

There are many different types of growth for any new idea or product. Typically, in the market economy growth is limited by the boundaries of an organisation, whereas in the social economy growth tends to be more diffuse, expanding through networks, multiplying and transforming across different actors. In this section we explore some of the theories relating to the adoption of new ideas and the factors that influence the speed of their uptake. In addition to which we consider the characteristics for scaling and replicating social innovations.

The way in which new ideas spread has been a subject of study for decades. The theoretical foundations for analysis were established in the book *The Diffusion of Innovations*, published by the rural sociologist Everett Rogers in 1962. Rogers proposed that four elements influence the spread of a new idea: the quality of the innovation itself; the communication channels or means by which messages get from one individual to another; time – the period required for the innovation to be adopted; and, finally, the social system in which the innovation is situated. He also broke the diffusion of an innovation down into the following five stages: 1) knowledge – an individual is exposed to an innovation, but lacks information and is not yet inspired to find out more; 2) persuasion – the individual is interested and actively seeks out more information; 3) decision – weighing up the advantages and disadvantages, the individual decides whether or not to take up the innovation; 4) implementation – the individual employs the innovation to a varying degree depending on the situation; and, 5) confirmation – the individual finalises the decision to continue using the innovation.

The process of social innovation may differ as the "client", who may need persuading to fund or support a given social innovation as described in the previous chapters, is not necessarily the "beneficiary". This means that two separate diffusion processes may be needed, one for the client and one for the beneficiary.

The diffusion of innovations

An additional contribution made by Rogers in his seminal publication was a description of the factors affecting the rate of adoption, which are useful to apply in the context of social innovation. Included among these are: the relative advantage of the innovation – the improvement it offers over previous and existing ideas, practices or technologies; compatibility – the degree to which the innovation fits into an individual's life (or in the case of social innovation, into the relevant social context); the scope for being trialled – how easily it can be experimented with (if a user is able to test an innovation, he or she may be more likely to adopt it); and observability – the extent to which the innovation is visible to others. The more visible an innovation is, the more likely it is that it will be communicated across networks. In recent years, the use of social networks has greatly enhanced the visibility and speed of uptake of all types of innovations.

Figure 30. Diffusion of innovation

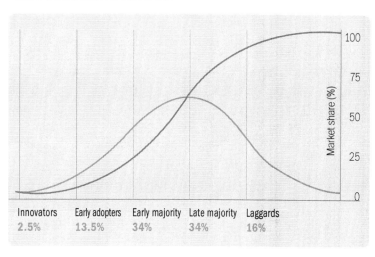

Groups of consumers who adopt a new technology (purple line), overall share of the market (grey line). Source: Rogers 2003

In the course of his study, Rogers traced the different groups of individuals involved in the process of adopting any new idea from the innovators themselves, followed by the early adopters, the early majority, then the later majority and finally the laggards, as illustrated in Figure 30. However, a limitation of Rogers's Diffusion of Innovation model is that, firstly, it does not consider the fluidity of many innovation processes, for example in the technological field where there may be multiple iterations of a particular product at the different stages of its development. Secondly, it fails to address the involvement of the users and multiple other actors in the design and development process, as is the case for many social innovations and above all in open innovation.

Generative diffusion

The concept of scaling has its roots in the manufacturing sector and is based on the application of the mathematical logic of economies of scale to reduce operating costs and increase margins through a linear process. However, in the case of social innovation, where a social objective takes precedence over any financial objectives, rapid diffusion is favoured achieving more advantageous profit margins or limiting costs. In contrast to the linear manufacturing model the social innovation process is often more organic with ideas adapting as they spread, rather than growing in a single form. Murray *et al.* have used the term *generative diffusion* to describe the process of the spread of social innovation; it is generative because the adoption of a social innovation will take on new shapes and forms, rather than replicate an identical model, and "diffusion" as it spreads; indeed, sometimes it will move chaotically along multiple paths. Furthermore, they describe the spread of social innovation as a *"more complex flow-like process of interaction and modification (...) analogous to the spread of a chemical liquid (...) also termed fission, contagion, translation and dissemination.*" The idea of micro-credits is a good example of generative diffusion; this innovative banking practice was initiated by Muhammad Yunus and the Grameen Bank, and later adopted and adapted by different organisations across the world, such as BRAC and ASA. It is now a concept that even mainstream banks are beginning to offer, albeit under very different circumstances to those that prompted the original idea.

Regardless of an innovation's type of growth, an important factor for its successful uptake is the guarantee of an effective supply and demand. On the supply side, it is important for the idea to have successfully demonstrated that it works, and on the demand side that individuals or organisations are willing to pay for it. In the case of social innovation, there are typically more resources invested in the supply side, such as grants, social venture capital and other financial mechanisms, which place an emphasis on measuring effectiveness, value for money and potential adaptations of the innovation to suit different contexts (Murray *et al.* 2010).

In parallel to the question of supply, it is necessary to stimulate demand for the product or service and this can be achieved in many ways. Firstly, through advocacy, awareness-raising and infor-mation campaigns, such as national health service campaigns to reduce smoking or promote healthy diets. Secondly, user groups and campaign groups stimulate demand for a particular activity, such as the bicycle group Critical Mass, which consists of self-organised local groups who take over the streets with bicycles once a month in different cities, raising awareness about diverse issues related to urban cycling. Another important mechanism used to stimulate demand for certain products are brands and certifications for fair trade and organic products. In addition to these, there are the social targets adopted by governments to stimulate demand, such as the UK's 10:10 campaign, launched in 2009 to encourage individuals, businesses and institu-tions to reduce their CO_2 emissions by 10% by 10th October 2010. Finally, media campaigns and government lobbying processes are alternative mechanisms used to influence the take-up of proposals from the social economy. The relational capacity of a given social innovation can help to influence the speed or effectiveness with which it becomes adopted and eventually accepted by mainstream society.

Organisational models for scaling social innovation

A social innovation's type of growth is influenced by the organisational model adopted, and in this regard there are various options available. The first, and perhaps simplest, type is the concept of scaling with its roots in the manufacturing sector, which (as has already been mentioned) is very common in the market economy, but surprisingly it is rarely applied to social innovations. NGOs and small social enterprises usually find growth difficult, in part for the financial reasons mentioned previously, but also be cause of the internal management changes that may need to be adopted and which affect leadership styles and organisational culture and accountability structures. They may also compromise the entity's overriding social objective in order to meet financial objectives. However, there a number of other organisational models used to facilitate the growth of social innovation and the following paragraphs discuss them with reference to key examples of their application.

Collaborations and partnerships are a typical structure used to cut across the different interfaces of the social economy discussed above. These collaborations may include public–private partnerships to address common goals, NGO–business partnership models or multi-sectoral networks. In all cases successful expansion of the social innovation depends on the conditions for the collaboration being right, as has been discussed earlier. An interesting example of this model being applied is the Communities of Practice (COP) run by the UK government body IDEA. These COPs are often used in public sector social innovation to bring together groups of people who share a common concern to pool knowledge and experience through a process of experiential learning.[82]

Spin-offs are another mechanism to spread social innovation, particularly from well-established businesses or universities with sufficient organisational capacity to support the process. Universities typically spin off a technological enterprise after establishing a product or service through internal R&D support, as was the case of Innova launched by the Universitat Politècnica de Catalunya (UPC).[83] In the private sector, the "Bunsha" method is a variant of the spin-off mechanism; a company director may pick a director from within the company to start a new venture and the company supports that venture with financial capital and other needs.

Mergers and acquisitions are also used in the social economy to help organisations grow not only in size, but also in terms of acquiring new technologies, capacities, diffusing risk and increasing efficiency. Age UK was set up from the merger of two age-related charities, Age Concern and Help the Aged, while Actuable, the Spanish online petition platform, was recently acquired by the larger organisation change.org.

Franchises are more common models for scaling up social innovation as they enable an idea to spread without the challenge of internal organisational growth. The School for Entrepreneurs, which was started in the UK, is a good example of this. There are now seven schools in the network; each pays a flat fee of £10,000 that covers a best-practice guide, quality standards, learning resources, a branded website, technical support, policy work, media relations and evaluation tools. The HUB network's[84] work and event centres for social entrepreneurs operate under a similar scheme, while another inspiring example is that of Riverford Organic Farms[85] which has franchised its distributors to create a regional network to deliver from its five sister farms, which enables it to keep the organisation's structure small and production local. Riverford now delivers organic vegetable boxes to 47,000 homes per week to areas across the UK.

---

82 The local government improvement and development initiative IDEA has a series of Communities of Practice for various topics which are now all accessible via the new Knowledge Hub: https://knowledgehub.local.gov.uk.

83 www.pinnova.upc.edu at the Technical University of Catalonia.

84 The HUB network is now in 25 countries: www.the-hub.net.

85 www.riverford.co.uk

Licences are another option for expanding an innovation. Using these, the social innovation is transformed into intellectual property and licensed for use to others. It should be noted that there have been mixed experiences of this model. Firstly, it is difficult (and costly) to protect intellectual property in court, and, secondly, putting a price on an innovation is an immediate barrier to reducing its potential spread.

Federations are a popular mechanism used in the social economy. Enthusiasts for a model are identified and given the know-how and, importantly, the autonomy to manage their own operations. This mechanism is used to facilitate the international expansion of many well-known organisations such as Greenpeace, Médecins Sans Frontières, as well as local groups such as the Federació Catalana d'ONG per al Desenvolupament (FCONGD, The Catalan Federation of NGOs for Development).

> Regardless of the type of organisational model adopted, there is a growing interest from a range of actors in transmitting relevant information to help stimulate uptake. The mechanisms used include thematic platforms such as the 350 climate change platforms, events, trade fairs, the media, associations and quasi-professional bodies, handbooks, guides and consultancy networks. The media play an especially important role as a transmitter of new ideas, as was illustrated by Jamie Oliver's "School Dinners" television series , which launched his "Feed Me Better" campaign which in turn gave a major stimulus for healthier eating in schools (Murray *et al.* 2010).

Box 15. The story of Aspire – a failed franchise

Of course, not all social innovations are able to scale with success and the type of growth model adopted is of key importance. Aspire, a British social enterprise which employed homeless people in a door-to-door sales business selling fair-trade products, is one example of how social franchises can fail. Aspire was launched in 1999 and supported by the Prince's Trust in order to help homeless people back into employment. In 2001, it was decided to expand the project through a franchise model; having a turnover of £1.6m, the enterprise secured an investment of £400,000. Unfortunately, by 2004 it had gone bankrupt.

The decision to franchise was taken in order to increase Aspire's purchasing power, reduce its costs and expand into new markets. However, soon after the franchises were set up, it became clear that the basic model was unsustainable. Sales were low, the product line limited and working with homeless people did not prove easy for the franchisees, which made it difficult to achieve the dual financial and social objectives. Faced with poor results from catalogue sales Aspire diversified into other activities – bike repairs and cleaning services, but this meant less energy was devoted to relationships with the franchisees and their work, and this dimension eventually became neglected.

Analysis of this case has shown that a franchise can only work if the original business model has already proven successful and has a strong brand. In addition there needs to be an ongoing and supportive relationship between franchisee and franchisor. Franchising is not a quick fix and is best suited to mature social ventures.

Source: Jarvis 2006

Control versus speed of uptake

A factor that is seen to influence the uptake of a social innovation is the level of control the social entrepreneur or founder of the innovation has over the product or process. A study of the spread of the Self-Funded Communities model shows evidence of a reverse correlation between the level of control over a particular social innovation and the speed of uptake (Murillo 2010). The model consists of six levels of control exercised over a particular innovation. They range from a centralised system with total control over the brand, implementation and monitoring to an established concept that can be used by any group. As illustrated in Figure 31, the model suggests that the less control over the idea, the faster its uptake.

Figure 31. Control versus speed trade-off

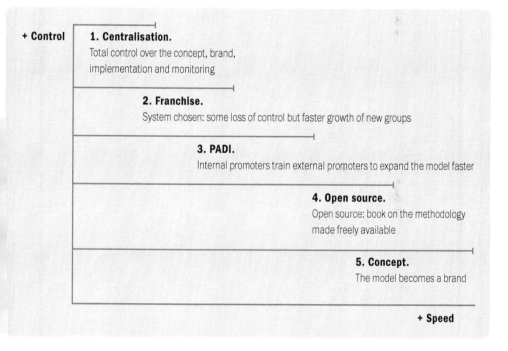

Source: Murillo 2011

Emergence theory

Finally, we will now consider the concept of emergence, which has been used since the times of Aristotle to explore the way complex systems and patterns arise out of a multiplicity of relatively simple interactions. It has been developed in response to the successes and failures of reductionist approaches to science and the realisation that all laws of nature cannot be reduced to the laws of physics alone. The application of emergence theory to social innovation has focused on the process by which separate local efforts connect with each other as networks, strengthen as practice-based communities, and finally develop new systems at a completely different level of scale. This theory is inspired by natural patterns that show how systems do not develop through planning or *top-down* hierarchies, but rather through a multitude of interconnected actions that result in something that is far greater than could ever be imagined by calculating the sum of the individual parts of the system. Rather than solely investing in individual entrepreneurs, fostering social innovation by connecting entrepreneurs with other like-minded people could have far greater impact, because it creates the conditions for networks and, ultimately, the potential for systemic change as described in the table below (Wheatley 2010).

Box 16. The life cycle of emergence theory

Stage 1
There are more and more coalitions, alliances and networks forming across the world to create social change. They are fluid in nature with members moving in and out of them. They are essential for the first stage of emergence.

Stage 2
Communities of practice: networks make it possible for individuals to find others engaged in similar work and form smaller, self-organised groups. These groups differ from the networks because people make a commitment to be there for one another and serve the needs of others on the basis of an intentional need to advance practice in their field.

Stage 3
Systems of influence: the third stage can never be predicted as it is the sudden appearance of a system that has real power and influence; pioneering efforts that had hovered at the periphery become the norm.

Source: Wheatley 2010

———

Key references

Dees, G., Battle Anderson, B., & Wei-skillern, J. (2004)
Scaling Social Impact: Strategies for Spreading Social Innovations.
Stanford Social Innovation Review.

Rogers, E. (1962)
Diffusion of Innovations. New York: Free Press.

Murray, R., Caulier-Grice, J., & Mulgan, G. (2010)
The Open Book of Innovation. The Young Foundation and NESTA.

Mulgan, G., Ali, R., Halkett, R., and Sanders, B. (2007)
In and Out of Sync: The Challenge of Growing Social Innovations. London: NESTA.

Murillo, D., & Salsas, J. (2010)
SFC. Globalising a Social Entrepreneurship Project. ESADE.

Emerson, J. (2003)
The Blended Value Map: Tracking the Intersects and Opportunities of Economic, Social and Environmental Value Creation.
www.blendedvalue.org

Tracey, P., & Jarvis, O. (2006)
An Enterprising Failure. Why a Promising Social Enterprise Collapsed.
Stanford Social Innovation Review, Spring 2006.

Wheatley, P., & Frieze, D. (2006)
Lifecyle of Emergence. Using Emergence to Take Social Innovations to Scale.
Berkana Institute.

4

Some insights on social innovation: from practice to theory

The world's social problems are so complex and so diverse that there will never be a "one size fits all" model for social innovation. The very nature of social innovation as a new, better way of solving social problems means that it is not even in the interest of social innovation advocates to create tidy definitions or frameworks, but rather to create environments that allow for the process of creative destruction with a social purpose to prosper. The value of our variables is that they help define those environments. Some of the questions they help to answer are: is there a strategy for long-term financial viability in place? What type of innovation model is being adopted? What is the relationship between different sectors and is there sufficient freedom to scale up the innovation?

> The following pages describe what we have learned about the relevance of these five variables from the selected inspiring initiatives. We also consider how useful they are as parameters to understand whether a given social innovation is best placed to meet its social objectives and bring about systemic change. In other words, can these variables be used as indicators for measuring the potential of any given social innovation?

Social impact and different motivations for measurement

All four cases are making a positive social impact and to varying degrees are bringing about systemic change. This is made evident particularly in the case of Avaaz and the Barcelona Food Bank, as these initiatives prioritise measurement as part of their culture of organisational excellence. In both cases, they provide easily digestible figures to inform members and donors respectively of progress towards their mission. The Bank's *Gran Recapte* campaign is built around clear targets and achievements, which are measured in terms of kilos of food redistributed to those in need. Avaaz's campaigns are likewise often based around the number of signatories for a certain petition and so are also easy to measure.

Beyond the quantitative data, both organisations use simple clear language and targeted messages to communicate their impact. For example, at the end of the year, an email from the founder of Avaaz is sent out highlighting key achievements, and a comprehensive press pack is released by the Barcelona Food Bank. As both organisations depend on a large number of individuals to support and fund their activity, it is important to convey a series of clear messages that resonate with a large cross-section of society.

While there is a host of elaborate reporting mechanisms available to help measure and manage social impact as described in earlier sections, these two organisations do not use such mechanisms. Instead, they provide simple financial statements and basic information on their mission and demonstrate their progress towards reaching their targets on their websites. Simplicity is therefore a key element in their attempt to transmit the social impact generated by their actions.

Measurement of the potential impact of its interventions is also a priority for the Behavioural Insights Team. An important part of the Team's core philosophy is the need for robust testing of whether a given policy intervention will achieve its social objective. It is for this reason that considerable resources, time and sophisticated methodologies, such as randomised control testing, are deployed. The recipients of the information generated are often government departments, which will need convincing by sound scientific evidence before undertaking a particular intervention. In addition, the continued existence of the Team depends on the generation of proof that the approaches being undertaken are successful.

The measurement of social impact from the exchange networks is somewhat different, partly because they have a very different funding model. There are no salaried staff and infrastructure costs are kept to a minimum, as the networks are based on the free exchange of goods and knowledge. As a result, funders do not play a prominent role, with only occasional small public grants used for a specific project, such as a new website or the allocation of physical space for markets and workshops. This means that, at present, there is little motivation to measure and communicate impact, and all resources are targeted towards delivering the services provided.

Insights into social impact measurement

How social impact is measured is very closely linked to an organisation's funding model; reporting motivations will differ if the organisation depends on multiple individual donations or has strategic partnerships with one or two key organisations. Also, social impact measurement will depend on the internal organisational culture; where there is a culture focused on performance and efficiency measurement it is likely to be more robust, and where the organisational culture is looser and more organic, there are fewer resources put into performance measurement.

Cross-sector collaboration and an increasingly proactive household economy

All of the four cases depend on a series of interactions at the different interfaces between the market, grant, government and household economies. However, each of the case studies operates in a slightly different sphere within the so-called hybrid economy.

The Behavioural Insights Team and the Barcelona Food Bank rely on the market's involvement as a means to reach the household economy and both elaborate sophisticated partnership models to achieve this. Engagement with supermarkets to influence individuals' consumer behaviour is a good example of this, either to buy more healthy food in the case of the Behavioural Insights Team or to donate food to others in the case of the Barcelona Food Bank. A shared agenda, continued communication, common measuring tools and a backbone of support is important for these partnerships.

Another insight gained from studying these cases is that boundaries, roles and responsibilities between the different sectors are becoming increasingly blurred. Business practices are penetrating social enterprises, as is seen in Avaaz and the Barcelona Food Bank's cultures of efficiency and effectiveness. The application of knowledge that markets have been using for years such as behavioural psychology to a government programme is another example of this cross-fertilisation of ideas and resources.

Finally, the role of the household economy appears to be more and more important for social innovation, with increasing peer-to-peer relationships used to bring about social change. In many cases, initiatives operate without any support from the government, market or grant economies. Avaaz is a clear example of this, as it is sustained entirely by support from individuals and is entirely independent of the grant or government subsidy. Similarly, the Barcelona Exchange Networks operate within the context of mutual action between individuals from the household economy.

Insights into cross-sector collaboration

There are multiple opportunities for interaction across the different interfaces of the market, grant, household and state economies and each social innovation manages these in a particular way depending on their objectives. There is, however, a growing trend of social innovation arising from individual interactions across the household economy, ranging from local exchange networks to global campaigning platforms and in some cases these operate independently of the state or market economy.

Financial sustainability and innovative ways of achieving it

The four case studies reveal how social organisations, just as all organisations, thrive on efficiency, transparency and measurable outcomes for sustained growth. Avaaz, the Behavioural Insights Team and the Barcelona Food Bank demonstrate this clearly. The Barcelona Exchange Network follows a slightly different model, its efforts to achieve organisational efficiency and growth have occurred more slowly, which is most probably due to its completely horizontal (flat) structure. Financial sustainability is achieved in this case by a complete reliance on popular support, with very limited amounts of money being involved in the networks' organisation of the exchanges of goods and services.

Avaaz, the Behavioural Insights Team and the Barcelona Food Bank have all ingeniously side-stepped what was earlier described as the capital challenge – the difficulty many social organisations face in trying to gain access to financial capital in order to grow and scale up their operations. Each of the case studies has adopted a unique strategy. Avaaz has built its model on having a massive membership base, making fundraising as simple as three emails a year to cover operational costs. In addition, its overheads are kept to a minimum and the organisation operates according to a philosophy of maximum efficiency. The Behavioural Insights Team has an entirely different approach, seeking out major cost savings or sources of revenue by applying behavioural economics to achieve more effective tax payments, debt collection and other activities that save the government money. Finally, the Barcelona Food Bank achieves economic sustainability through a unique combination of volunteerism, austerity, efficiency and avoidance of the use of money. Nothing is bought and nothing is sold, food comes into the bank free and is distributed free.

Curiously, while we have noted a proliferation of financial institutions and grant mechanisms to support social innovation, it is important to highlight that these four cases have all built their financial models independently of the grant economy and, apart from the Behavioural Insight Team, independently of government support as well.

Insights into economic sustainability

Different types of fundraising models are used for different types of social innovation with a shift away from the support offered by grants or governments towards models of economic sustainability developed on the basis of the interactions of many individuals. In addition to this, social innovation can thrive if operational excellence, austerity and efficiency are adopted, which is an example of how commercial practices are penetrating the social economy.

Innovation types and the right conditions

While, previously, social innovation may have been said to come from key individuals, "wild spirits", or resource-rich organisations with the capacity to invest in research and development, the case studies in this book show an increasing diversity of sources of social innovation. Avaaz and the Big Food Collection are led by visionary individuals with a clear social purpose, however, the Behavioural Insights Team was the result of a more organic process, which involved a growing culture of applying behavioural science to public policy along with early academic experiments carried out in the US.

Some of the cases are more radical than others in terms of their innovation style. The innovation behind Avaaz can be described as radical – as the first global petition-making platform of its kind. Avaaz achieves in days what traditional civil society organisations may have taken years to do. The Barcelona Food Bank is also achieving radical systemic change; the food industry is beginning to change its practice and now, rather than throwing food away, delivers it to the food bank. The Barcelona Exchange Networks and the work of the Behavioural Insights Team are more incremental in their approach, both effecting more subtle behavioural change over longer periods of time.

The four case studies all use open innovation approaches, some being slightly more "open" than others. User input in the development of the innovation is one element of open innovation that has been adopted to varying degrees. This aspect is at the core of the exchange networks, where the users are the protagonists in the design of any given activity. In the case of the Barcelona Food Bank's Big Food Collection campaign volunteer coordinators are also given a key role in developing the campaign and are given key responsibilities for its implementation. In the case of Avaaz user input is less open and is carried out through annual user surveys.

In terms of open innovation the Behavioural Insights Team can be considered open on the macro scale as the Team's results are published and widely publicised across different government departments so that different units will adopt their own behavioural strategies. As a result each department has adopted a slightly different approach and mechanism for this purpose. However, on the micro scale during the innovation testing phase, the system is totally closed and users are completely unaware that they are involved in a social experiment.

Insights into innovation

While an open innovation approach appears to be essential to enable rapid growth of a social innovation, this alone does not guarantee its success. Some of the other favourable conditions for radical innovation are strong leadership, a complete understanding of and access to the relevant information, and good relationships with the relevant actors. From a societal perspective, it is relevant to highlight that success in social innovation practices derives to a great extent from their capacity to be transferred from organisation to organisation and from country to country. In this light the type of innovation (open versus closed) is paramount in facilitating or preventing the expansion of any given social innovation.

Mechanisms to successfully scale social innovation

With most social innovation, there is a need to scale up activity, but rather than replicate an identical model it is often better to allow for a more organic, diffuse form of growth. This is clear from the Barcelona exchange networks, which have grown freely and organically without any financial implication, licensing model, intellectual property or other constraint. A free flow of information has been important in this process and the development of websites has facilitated this.

Likewise, the Behavioural Insights Team's work has spread from one government department to another and from one city council to another. Information has been made available where possible, through a series of seminars and reports on the trials and initiatives carried out. A constant reiterative process of "trial, test and adapt" has further helped the model to be successfully extended to different parts of government.

The Barcelona Food Bank and its Big Food Collection campaign stems from a different type of growth model. In Spain, the Food Banks operate under a federal model, whereby any city is free to start up their own Bank; however, they do so according to the format agreed by the Federation. For example, within the Spanish framework, Seville's Big Food Collection campaign was started with support from Barcelona. This system may not be the most appropriate to scale up operations quickly as was shown by the attempt to set up a national Big Food Collection across Spain, even though the national model has been shown to be successful in other countries, such as Portugal, where two Big Food Collections are run each year.

Avaaz is the exception to this rule, as it has undergone massive organisational growth instead of being replicated organically in different formats. However, the inspiration in this case is based on the strength of the Avaaz brand, under which all its activities operate. However, it should be noted that, although Avaaz appears as a single entity, in reality the organisation is a complex network of interrelated campaign teams working on different issues in different countries.

Insights into scalability

Not all social innovations grow according to a process of generative diffusion and change and adapt as they grow. Some may experience controlled but very successful organisational growth while others might spread more organically. In general, where there is a restriction on the application of the social innovation in a new context, this can slow down uptake and scalability.

To conclude, the five chosen variables can be used as parameters to help map a route for effective social innovation. They present a set of key questions for practitioners, civil society groups, governments, funders and academics: what is the potential social impact of the initiative and how can it be measured? Is the initiative financially viable in the long term? Who are the different actors involved and how are they involved? What type of innovation is used and what is the potential for it to be scaled up? However, these variables should by no means be seen as restrictive, since social innovation by definition is constantly generating new paradigms, breaking boundaries and destroying old ideas and assumptions. In this light, we hope this book serves to enrich the debate and inspire others to take one of the many pathways to stimulate systemic change.

———

Appendix 1. Definitions of "Social Innovation"

Phills et al., 2008
A novel solution to a social problem that is more effective, efficient, sustainable or just than existing solutions and for which the value created accrues primarily to society as a whole rather than private individuals.

Murray, Caulier-Grice & Mulgan, 2010, p. 3
We define social innovations as new ideas (products, services and models) that simultaneously meet social needs and create new relationships or collaborations. In other words, they are innovations that are both good for society and enhance society's capacity to act.

Bacon, Faizullah, Mulgan & Woodcraft, 2008
We use the term "social innovation" to refer to new ideas (products, services and models) developed to fulfil unmet social needs. Many are supported by the public sector, others by community groups and voluntary organisations. Social innovation is not restricted to any one sector or field.

Mulgan, Tucker, Ali & Sanders, 2007
Innovative activities and services that are motivated by the goal of meeting a social need and that are predominantly developed and diffused through organisations whose primary purposes are social.

Mumford, 2002
The generation and implementation of new ideas about how people should organise interpersonal activities, or social interactions, to meet one or more common goals.

Marcy & Mumford, 2007
New ideas about social systems and social interactions, while rare, can have a tremendous impact on our lives and world.

Westley, 2008
Social innovation is an initiative, product or process or program that profoundly changes the basic routines, resource and authority flows or beliefs of any social system.

Eric Young, cited by Pearson, 2007
Social innovation is not just about improving the innovative capacity of social organisations. Rather, it is about innovations in our capacity to organise social and financial resources to achieve large-scale social impact.

Gerometta, Haussermann & Longo, 2005
Three core dimensions: the satisfaction of human needs (content dimension); changes in social relations especially with regard to governance (process dimension); and an increase in the socio-political capability and access to resources (empowerment dimension).

Nilsson, 2003
A social innovation as a significant, creative and sustainable shift in the way that a given society dealt with a profound and previously intractable problem such as poverty, disease, violence or environmental deterioration.

Centre for Social Innovation, Toronto

Social innovation refers to new ideas that resolve existing social, cultural, economic and environmental challenges for the benefit of people and planet. A true social innovation is system-changing – it permanently alters the perception, behaviours and structures that previously gave rise to those challenges... Even more simply, a social innovation is an idea that works for the public good.

Pol & Ville, 2009, p. 881

"Social innovation" is a term that almost everyone likes, but nobody is quite sure what it means. Some academics would like to abandon the notion of social innovation altogether, arguing that it adds nothing to what we know about innovation and is too vague to be useful.

Sotarauta, 2009, p. 623

Perhaps it [social innovation] is one of those concepts that can only be framed and used as an analytical tool as well as one can but not exhaustively defined. It goes without saying that the concept of social innovation provides not only a seductively topical, but also a positively wholesome counterweight to more technologically orientated literature. The problem, however, is that when one presses harder to pin down the idea, its inherent appeal and the search for conceptual clarity and precision is tested by theoretical complexity, ambiguity and frustrating conceptual flexibility.

European Commission Innovation Union, 2010

Social innovation is about tapping into the ingenuity of charities, associations and social entrepreneurs to find new ways of meeting social needs which are not adequately met by the market or the public sector. It can help bring about the behavioural changes needed to tackle the major societal challenges, such as climate change. Social innovations empower people and create new social relationships and models of collaboration. They are thus innovative in themselves and good for society's capacity to innovate.

Saul, 2011

Social innovation is about innovating creative, market-based solutions to social problems that result in high growth, profitable business opportunities.

———

Appendix 2. Social Innovation Hotspots Directory

There is a growing sector of different types of organisations with an interest in stimulating, supporting and observing social innovation around the world. In this table we highlight some of the organisations, foundations, academic centres, international sharing platforms and communities that support social innovation.

Foundations and organisations

NAME	BASED	SCALE	FUNDING	NETWORKING	SUPPORT SERVICES	RESEARCH
The Skoll Foundation	US	Global	X	X	X	X
Ashoka	US	Global	X	X	X	
Acumen Fund	US	Global	X	X		
The Young Foundation	UK	UK and increasingly international		X	X	X
The Schwab Foundation for Social Entrepreneurship	US	Global	X	X	X	X
Unreasonable Institute	US	Global	X	X	X	
Root Cause	US	US		X	X	X
Echoing Green	US	US	X	X	X	
Centre for Social Innovation	Canada	Canada (with a focus on Toronto)		X	X	X

International platforms and communities

NAME	BASED	NEWS & INFORMATION	NETWORKING	RESEARCH	CO-WORKING SPACE
Social Innovation Exchange	UK	X	X	X	
Asian Social Innovation Exchange	Asia	X	X	X	
Australian Social Innovation Exchange	Australia	X	X	X	
Social Innovation Europe	Europe	X	X	X	
Social Edge	US	X	X		X

Academic hubs

NAME	BASED	TEACHING	RESEARCH	TRAINING / INCUBATION
Center for Social Innovation, Stanford Graduate School of Business	US	X	X	
Skoll Centre for Social Entrepreneurship, Saïd Business School, the University of Oxford	US	X	X	
Institute for Social Innovation, ESADE	Spain	X	X	X
Social Enterprise Initiative, Harvard Business School	US			
Social Enterprise Knowledge Network	Latin America	X	X	
Center for the Advancement of Social Entrepreneurship, Fuqua School of Business, Duke University	US	X	X	
Social Innovation Centre, INSEAD	France	X	X	
Centre de Recherche sur les Innovations Sociales	Canada	X	X	
School for Social Entrepreneurs	UK, Australia, Canada	X		X

For Product Safety Concerns and Information please contact our EU
representative GPSR@taylorandfrancis.com Taylor & Francis Verlag GmbH,
Kaufingerstraße 24, 80331 München, Germany

Printed and bound by CPI Group (UK) Ltd, Croydon, CR0 4YY

04/05/2025

01860548-0001